Peter Malatesta

PRENTICE-HALL, INC., Englewood Cliffs, NJ 07632

Party Politics by
Peter Malatesta

Address inquiries to Prentice-Hall, Inc.,
Englewood Cliffs, N.J. 07632
Printed in the United States of America
Prentice-Hall International, Inc., London
Prentice-Hall of Australia, Pty. Ltd., Sydney
Prentice-Hall of Canada, Ltd., Toronto
Prentice-Hall of India Private Ltd., New Delhi
Prentice-Hall of Japan, Inc., Tokyo
Prentice-Hall of Southeast Asia Pte. Ltd., Singapore
Whitehall Books Limited, Wellington, New Zealand

10 9 8 7 6 5 4 3 2 1

Library of Congress Cataloging in Publication Data

Malatesta, Peter.
Party politics.

1. Washington (D.C.)—Social life and customs—date. 2. Malatesta, Peter. 3. Journalists—Washington (D.C.)—Biography. 4. Washington (D.C.)—Biography. I. Title.
F200.M33 975.3'04 81-11935
AACR2

ISBN 0-13-652552-0

Dedicated to Mildred and John,
who taught me to take life more seriously than myself.

An Acknowledgment to the Editor:

For two years Tom Lauria was committed to the occasionally staggering task of shaping, editing, and reconstructing a decade's worth of material. His humor, insight, and determination proved to be invaluable, and I am deeply grateful for both the quality and quantity of his efforts.

PM

Ten years of champagne and smoke were in my eyes that May night in 1978. Exhausted and pale from days of intense preparation for the party, I staggered into my restaurant, realizing there were still twenty-odd final touches to attend to before the two hundred and fifty guests arrived.

I just wasn't ready for Lucille Ball, standing at the maitre d' station with menus in hand. With perfect gravity, she asked me if I wanted a table for two, requested my name, and held out her hand like a maitre d' on the take.

Chagrined and dazed, I asked, "What's happening? What are you doing here so soon? The White House doesn't break up 'til seven."

"Oh, Peter," she laughed, "the old place ain't what it used to to be. . . . White wine, yuk! Next it'll be tea and peanut-butter sandwiches."

Her husband, Gary Morton, came up from behind me with a rousing slap on my back and, still foggy-eyed, I saw the bar filling up. Danny Thomas appeared out of nowhere. "Malatesta! My God! By now, you must be older than I am." Measuring the way I felt against his relaxed smile, I think he was right.

I scurried up to the bar, hoping a quick scotch would extinguish my desire to sneak back out, catch a nap, and try my entrance over again. I ran into Les Brown and his wife, Claire, both of whom I've known since childhood, maybe a hundred years ago. "Well, it's Peter Malaprop," he said, grinning, remembering the nickname he gave me when I was still a young buck in the Air Force.

2

“How was the White House, Les?” I asked, grasping for conversation.

“Ah,” he grunted. “I was dying for a real drink!”

Looking over his shoulder into the main entrance foyer, I saw a flock of limos had pulled up, with onlookers and cameras everywhere zooming in on Elliott and Jennifer Gould, David Soul, and Mac Davis. Well, this is it! I thought to myself. You’re on, baby! Pull yourself together and go do your thing.

I was hosting a seventy-fifth birthday party for Bob Hope, *the* entertainer of the twentieth century—a man who, as my Uncle Bob, had had a tremendous influence on my life since my mother and father moved from New York to Los Angeles when I was still a child. Now, my restaurant, Peter’s in Alexandria, Virginia, across the Potomac River from the National Capital, was a perfect and fitting place to fete this man who triggered my life into a remarkable and, for the most part, interesting experience. Thanks for the memories, indeed!

It was also a birthday celebration for my mother’s sister, Dolores Hope. After my parents, Dolores is my most devoted mentor. She has always kept an eye on my life, celebrated my successes, and comforted me when I felt I was alone in the world. Throughout my life, she has stood by as my confessor, my guardian angel, my crony, occasionally my banker, and always my friend. Along with much else, I owed this moment to the tall, graceful woman who had long ago taken a bedazzled nephew under her wing.

The limos continued to roll up to the main entrance of Peter’s. A crowd of two thousand enthusiastically acknowledged many of their favorite personalities as they entered: Fred MacMurray and his wife, June Haver; Pearl Bailey; Elizabeth Taylor; Dorothy Lamour; Bert Convy; Lucie Arnaz; Charo; Charles Nelson Reilly; Shields and Yarnell; Jim Henson and Frank Oz of the Muppets; Generals Omar Bradley, Jimmy Doolittle, and Westy Westmoreland; the Leonard Firestones; the Peter Graces; the W. Clement Stones—old show business, new show business, the professional and business arenas, military and political leaders, family, and just plain longtime friends—all there to honor a couple they loved.

When Bob and Dolores arrived, the crowd roared with pleasure. The mayor of Alexandria remarked proudly, “This is the largest social event in northern Virginia since George Washington’s Birthday Ball!” The Hopes beamed as they greeted the crowd and entered the restaurant to be welcomed wildly again, this time by their assembled guests. Moving from handshakes to kisses to hugs, I knew they were pleased.

As I escorted them through the throng of familiar faces, I realized that this event was affecting me in a way that went beyond just the wonderful glow anyone feels when hosting a nearly perfect party. It suddenly seemed to me to be filled with symbolism of a very personal kind, as though Bob's birthday were giving me a perspective on the patterns in my life and the scheme of things. The party's guests were more than just reminders of various people, places, and events that I had known; they seemed to sum up my whole life—a life that had somehow become inextricably involved in giving parties.

Taking stock of it all, looking back over forty years, from a fresh kid on a bike in North Hollywood to a man hosting an historic birthday for his favorite aunt and uncle, I realized how many times I'd gone through the social mill in the pursuit of happiness—especially during these last ten years in Washington, when my entertaining had subtly changed from a pleasant pastime to full-scale vocation. So this party may have been a seventy-fifth gala for the Hopes, but it was also a portrait of a considerable journey traveled by a certain short man with a big smile.

Chapter One

Although she was hardly described as a "December bride," Linda Hope's wedding did fall in the last month of 1968. The ceremony and reception promised to be an extravaganza, even by Hollywood standards. At Dolores' request, I was to act as chief of protocol, coordinating the church seating arrangements for the family and numerous VIPs.

With all their wealth, Bob and Dolores Hope have never been pretentious, and the thought of a media-event wedding didn't thrill them. But if daughter Linda wanted it that way. . So, in the end, the Hope guest list read just as you'd expect it to: the Bing Crosbys, the Clem Stones, the Ronald Reagans, the Johnny Mercers . . . a hundred et ceteras. You name 'em, they were there.

As I surveyed the list, there was only one surprise—"Spiro T. Agnew, Vice President Elect." I made a mental note. Of all the guests present, I was going to have to make a special effort to get to know Spiro Agnew.

Months earlier, at the Republican Convention in Miami, while working on the veiled vice-presidential bid of my good friend Senator John Tower, I had had a fleeting glimpse of "Spiro Who?" but we were not introduced. I remembered him, however, because of a rather spooky incident that took place at the Palm Bay Club.

I had met a Republican crony of Tower's named Louise Gore, the GOP state chairman for Maryland. Gore was immensely knowledgable about the national political scene and was, in fact, the person who introduced Richard Nixon to the then-governor of Maryland, Spiro T. Agnew. Besides being an astute politician, Louise was a lot of fun. At the close of each day, she and her chum, Virginia Page, would rally with me at the Palm Bay Bar, where we'd hash over the day's activities, rumors, and gossip.

On the second day of our new friendship—the evening before Nixon was to name his running mate—Louise turned to me and, in a clear, serious voice, said, "Our friend John Tower is *not* going to be picked as Nixon's Veep; Spiro Agnew will be named. Peter, although you don't know Ted Agnew now, you will soon be deeply involved with him and will play a very important role in his life."

I was flabbergasted and turned quickly to Virginia Page. "Peter," she said, "Louise doesn't *know* anything more than you do, but she does have remarkable psychic insight. Something about you triggered it; don't laugh." I did, but not heartily.

Louise's eerie prediction kept running through my mind for weeks, right up to the Hope wedding. If Tower had been chosen, of course I would have been involved; but this guy from Maryland and I were strangers. Hell, I don't even know anyone from Maryland except Louise, I thought. But now I'd see for myself.

After a lengthy but beautiful service at St. Charles Roman Catholic Church in North Hollywood, the twelve ushers in high hats and gray cutaways, the maids of honor, and five hundred guests returned with the bridal party to the Hope family estate. The Hopes' spread in Toluca Lake is a choice piece of real estate tucked away on Moorpark Street. Bought in the forties, situated amid a grove of walnut trees, the home has been expanded into a 27-room mansion, with guest quarters, a golfing hole, a huge swimming pool, tiered gardens, and a free-standing office building housing Hope's files and memorabilia.

The endless receiving line moved at a snail's pace as the father of the bride dutifully quipped with each guest. I slipped in the back way, wandered over to the pool area and, as if by destiny, came face-to-face with the next Vice President of the United States. Tall, erect, and immaculately groomed, Agnew stood talking to his senior aide, Art Sohmer. God! I thought, this towering, silver-haired man even *looks* like a vice president.

I flashed my best smile and stuck out my hand. "Hi, Mr. Vice President! I'm Peter Malatesta, Linda's cousin."

With a tight smile, squinty eyes, and a firm handshake, Agnew returned my greeting, and before long we were chatting like old acquaintances. At first, his inquiries were prosaic enough—he wanted to know the details of Linda and her husband's courtship, the history of the Hope house, how many members of the family were able to make the wedding. Then the conversation, by my design or his, eventually turned to my background. I rattled off my various public relations and political efforts for the Republican party, and Agnew listened with what I thought was more than passive curiosity. Finally, our first conversation wound down with a lighthearted discussion of his fondness for Palm Springs, California, which he had visited once while governor of Maryland.

I casually commented that the desert was at its best during the spring and suggested that after the rigamarole of the inauguration Palm Springs might be a nice place to relax for a few days. Agnew nodded approvingly. Art Sohmer and I exchanged business cards, and I took my leave when a dozen or so guests wandered by, recognized Agnew and, with obvious interest, wanted to meet him.

As I watched the tall vice-presidential figure move through the milling crowd, I couldn't help noticing, as I often had before, the almost reverent awe a Washington VIP commands from Tinseltown. I remembered how some nine years earlier a star-packed Hope New Year's Eve party was turned gaga when Richard Nixon, then Vice President, arrived amidst blaring sirens, security, and scurrying Secret Service. To me, Washington had always been a powerful and remotely mysterious capital, and I often fantasized being a part of it. Hollywood was no longer a big deal to me.

Meandering through the winding, green hills of North Hollywood as a child, I thought celebrityhood was a way of life. I went with my pal Jack Haley, Jr., to visit his dad, the Tin Man, on the set of the film *The Wizard of Oz.* It was on the stage of Bob Hope's NBC radio show that I met my good friend-to-be Frank Sinatra. I cherished a dapper little cocker spaniel called Blondie that my friend Gary Crosby's mother, Dixie Lee, gave me at Malibu Beach. As a wide-eyed caddy, I observed a wise-ass Howard Hughes break up a crap game at Lakeside Country Club with a million-dollar bet. If I didn't quite understand why everyone suddenly dropped their forks at dinner while listening to Uncle Bob's radio show when he said, "Meet me at the pawn shop and kiss me under the balls," I nevertheless stood with a lump in my throat on Christmas Eve as I watched our neighbors, the Bing Crosbys, flee their burning house.

7

My father, John Malatesta, owned a 32-acre golfing range, which at times had more stars on the practice tees than in either of the two bordering studios, Warner Brothers and Universal. Working after school, I'd listen for hours as ancient but alert Mack Sennett, in faded Bermuda shorts and a beat-up rain hat, would spin his yarns about the offstage antics of the Keystone Kops. I watched a sad and anxious Marilyn Monroe try desperately to learn a golf swing "because Joe would be so disappointed" if she didn't. I saw a lonely Bob Mitchum, with the collar of his jacket up, sulk about the tee aimlessly, trying to find his way out of the "reefer" charges. I caught hell when I cut class once to watch my idol, Ben Hogan, in the finals of the Los Angeles Open. Hogan had once taught me to change my swing from a natural lefthanded one to a more compact right, and there had been a picture of Ben on the front page of the Los Angeles *Times* the next day, with me practically under his nose.

Later on, in college, I had produced the Loyola ROTC Military Ball, recruiting Danny Thomas and Les Brown, and proudly made my entrance with a rising young star named Debbie Reynolds on my arm.

Even in the service, my life didn't change much. Personally chosen by Three-Star General Frank (Twelve O'Clock High) Armstrong to be his traveling aide, Second Lieutenant Peter Malatesta found himself in charge of The Chateau, a private, full-service hotel for full colonels and above in Anchorage, Alaska. It was also the "in" haunt for junketing congressmen, who always seemed to be inspecting Alaskan military operations during salmon season.

Later, as a hotshot young law student in Hollywood, I tooled around in both a black Cadillac convertible and a used twelve-cylinder racing Ferrari that I bought from singer Guy Mitchell, whose wife had told him, "It's the car or me." Or I would hang out in a little Italian joint called the Villa Capri with Bobby Darin and speculate about the potential success of his new release, "Mac the Knife."

Addicted as I was to the gaudy world of show-biz celebrities, it was probably inevitable that I should open my own P.R./advertising firm. I landed the Wham-O toy account and one night, after a snootful, took a corkscrew to a Hula Hoop, loaded it with BB pellets, and came up with the "Shoop-Shoop Hula Hoop." In a rambling, two-bedroom spread in North Hollywood, I teamed up with local TV personality Johnny Grant, and we constantly entertained visiting baseball greats whenever they came to town—Mickey Mantle, Roger Maris, Yogi Berra, and Stan Musial, to name a few—and then spiced up the party with the likes of Jayne Mansfield, Angie Dickinson, Keeley Smith, and Ruta Lee.

As the years passed, I had begun to edge my way into Republican politics, first as a go-fer for former Vice President Richard Nixon, then as an adviser to presidential candidate Barry Goldwater, and most recently as an operative for Senator John Tower's 1968 vice-presidential aspirations. But even these adventures somehow hadn't served to alleviate the growing dissatisfaction I was beginning to feel with my life.

Now, standing at Linda's wedding, I felt burned out. Bored with Hollywood P.R. and disinterested in a Richard Nixon presidency, I was preparing for an around-the-world trip on my sailboat, just to get out of the rut. Although I felt certain I would meet Spiro Agnew again, I could not possibly have guessed then how much he was going to change my life, nor could I have imagined the heady new world of power, politics, and parties to which he would give me access.

Even my wildest fantasies would fall short of reality. The experiences I shared in and out of Washington over the next ten years would be bizarrely fascinating, downright intoxicating to mind (and body), and, at times, would show me just how intense life's disappointments and disillusionments can be. I often learned more about myself and others than I ever really cared to know.

It took two years after the Hope wedding for me to get to my White House office, but during this incubation period I found a new career being nurtured by one social gathering after another. I began to evaluate consciously what parties were really all about and how people used them. Looking past the booze, the buffet, and the comradery, there are always subtle intrigues at work that are far more important than surface frivolity. I started to understand why certain people who weren't particularly exciting were invited to a seemingly fun-only party. I also began to see why an outgoing and effervescent personality would sometimes jump to accept a party that promised to be thoroughly boring.

The reasons for this are as diverse as the motives. They range from a gnawing compulsion always to be seen where the action is, to the sledgehammer approach of a hardcore promoter, arm-wrestling his target into a quiet corner for "just a little business chat." After assessing my own quick rapport with Agnew, I decided it was time for me to take a lesson from the pros. After all, what was Agnew really doing at the Hope wedding in the first place? He didn't know Linda and had only met her father a couple of times. As a relative unknown from Maryland, he must have felt the need to broaden his political and social constituency. And what better way to do this than to cultivate the friendship of a mega-star like Hope? In a word, Agnew was "working" the party. On the other hand, since Bob's friend Richard Nixon couldn't make it, Hope sustained his ongoing political bravura by having the nation's number-two man present at his daughter's wedding. In any case, I now had a bona fide reason to go to the inauguration of Nixon-Agnew and, at least for a week, I would be 2,600 miles closer to the White House than I was standing in the gardens of Moorpark Street.

Sneaking into the Capital *alone* for the festivities wasn't in my game plan either. While I knew a dozen or so of the Republican hierarchy, I felt it would be more fun to arrive in the company of a recognizable personality. After all, I thought, Washington has always been celebrity-conscious, especially for Hollywood stars. And let's face it, Embassy Row is more apt to remember Peter Malatesta if he arrives with a household name. I was beginning to learn.

While attending some long-forgotten Beverly Hills bash prior to heading East, I had run into my buddy Chuck Connors, who was then filming a TV series called "The Rifleman" and, over a couple of drinks, I had talked him into coming back to the inauguration. "You've got to meet my newest 'best friend,' Spiro T.!" Chuck was all for that. He and I then recruited another chum who knew his way around Washington—flamboyant restaurateur Jay Fiondello. Thus prepared, we headed for Washington.

The 1969 inauguration was a Republican Mardi Gras with coronation overtones. The elephant had risen in triumph from the humiliation it had suffered in 1964. "Horatio" Nixon had overcome his sixth crisis and Spiro Agnew, a new white knight, spokesman for the middle class, and baiter of the elite, had arrived. Our happy trio, Chuck, Jay, and myself, were caught up in the excitement of the moment. We went from drink to buffet to limousine. Chuck played his role perfectly as a personable six-foot-six cowboy movie star, while Peter, his five-foot-eight Italian sidekick, had a ball.

10

I crossed paths for a second time with Spiro Agnew at a reception given for him by the Texas delegation—our invitations courtesy of Senator Tower. The Vice President and I exchanged brief pleasantries and he told me that I would be hearing from his office whenever he was next coming to California. My mood was jubilant, almost euphoric! He *did* remember me, but more important, I had a hunch I was about to be his man in California.

I followed up that second meeting with a letter, and the Vice President promptly and warmly responded. I called Art Sohmer on a regular basis, just to keep that pilot light on. In March 1969, I received a call from Sohmer that the Vice President was interested in visiting Palm Springs after a speech in Los Angeles. Did I have any ideas? (Ah, I began to smell the roses!)

My first call, of course, was to Uncle Bob. He was delighted that Agnew was coming but was unable to accommodate him at his home because of prior commitments to other guests. With Hope's house unavailable, I now had a free rein to come up with another facility that would let Agnew know my contacts and resources reached out further than just the Hopes.

During a round of golf at the El Dorado Country Club outside Palm Springs, Leonard Firestone told me of the availability of former President Eisenhower's house, off the thirteenth tee. It was an ideal place to put the Vice President—quiet, secluded, and certainly symbolic. I called Washington, and Art Sohmer was delighted. He asked me if I would like to do advance work for the trip and, in fact, if I would like to stay with the Vice President while he was at El Dorado. Stunned, but not silent, I replied, "Yes, that would be an honor."

Advancing the Vice President of the United States for the first time is akin to Alice's first day in Wonderland. Working with the experienced teams of Secret Service agents, White House communications men, and local police is the ultimate experience in efficiency. Every detail is covered in writing, from the moment the man is to set foot on the ground until his departure. Everyone who will come into contact with the Vice President in a service capacity is screened ahead of time. Motorcades are planned, streets are blocked off, every move is choreographed.

For the second day of Agnew's visit, I arranged a golf game for Agnew, Hope, Dr. Bill Voss (the Veep's traveling physician), and myself. After a slapstick eighteen holes of jokes and slices, we were invited to the Hopes' for dinner. An evening with them is always delightful, and this night was no exception. Although Dolores has a full-time cook and staff, she often loves to put on an apron, push back her sleeves, and make her famous antipasto salad, a meal in itself. While she toils in the kitchen, Bob will whip up a batch of fresh pineapple daquiris and deliver a nonstop stream of jokes. The only one I remember from that particular evening was his description of Agnew's golf swing: "It reminds me of Palmer—Betsy Palmer."

Dinner at the Hopes' desert home could either be sit-down or buffet, but in either case, very homey and informal. After-dinner hours are spent on conversation, listening to music, or watching television. This night found Spiro at the keyboard and Dolores singing renditions of "It Had To Be You" and "On a Clear Day." As a less jazzy Ella Fitzgerald, she's still a terrific singer. Following the musical interlude, Bob and Spiro drifted off for a chat and a walk in the cool desert night air. Soon after, we were back at El Dorado, ready to retire after a very satisfying day.

Agnew's first trip to Palm Springs as Vice President was a great success for him and for me. Sun and power in a relaxed setting are a hard pair to beat. It was the beginning of dozens of desert jaunts that would eventually see the Agnews buying a home there many years later.

By fall 1969, I was advancing all of the Vice President's trips to southern California. I had sold my interest in my advertising and public relations firm and was now biding time as a part-time P.R. consultant for a small West Coast petroleum company.

Although I had spent many hours with Agnew, I had never done so on my home turf. So now I planned a cozy sit-down dinner at my beach house at Marina-del-Rey. Agnew was in L.A. for a one-night speechmaking stopover, and it was a perfect time for a leisurely evening, complete with the Italian food I knew he loved. With Chopin for background and a gentle surf for relaxation, it would be a nice counterpart to his hectic agenda.

I rushed home late from the office and started throwing together his favorite entree, a basic marinara sauce. (The word *throwing* seems a little harsh, but any good Italian chef would never measure. Making sauce is like conducting music—you get a feel for it.) Routinely and somewhat abstractly, I went through the cupboards looking for the right seasonings. To my dismay I found I had lost track of the oregano. A good marinara sauce has to be pungent with oregano, so I started looking again. Not finding the spice, I dug into the separate kitchen setup of my roomer. I noticed he had some oregano; in fact, he had a big jar of it. Great! Right on track! I tossed in several healthy pinches and continued with my rushed dinner preparations.

For a dinner party that was supposed to be serene, this one really took off! Agnew was unusually animated and the conversation got downright heady. It was a thoroughly amusing evening, and for a spur-of-the-moment entertainment, things could not have gone better.

After Agnew had gone, and while I was still congratulating myself on my success, my boarder, Rob, came in and asked about the evening. He hadn't been present because we had a few standing rules about our life-styles. When I was entertaining biggies, I had to have the house to myself. Otherwise, some high-profile VIP was likely to run into Rob and his gang of beach friends hanging out in the living room. Rob always paid his rent on time and his personal socializing was no distraction to me.

So I recapped the evening, telling him how I had to rush home from the office and, as if I didn't have enough problems, I couldn't even find the damn oregano. "Thanks, Rob, but I finally used some of yours."

His face turned white. Very blankly he said, "Not the oregano on the third shelf?"

"Yeah."

He was panicked, absolutely panicked! He didn't know how I'd react, but he came out with it. It was good ol' Acapulco Gold. The best. Who could get mad? I started to laugh, and Rob took it easy.

A year or so later, Agnew and I were talking about marijuana and he made a comment about grass having this mysterious appeal to young people and how he had enjoyed his entire life without ever trying it.

I blushed inwardly and thought, You may think you never tried it, sir, but if you only knew. . . .

Of all the social vehicles available, a round of golf is as good as any to combine fun, relaxation, and bottom-line business. In my experience, I've seen more deals cut riding on a golf cart than in any boardroom or club. Agnew loved golf, and after a couple of good shots he was prepared to give almost any question benign consideration. Conversely, a bad round for Agnew could give his staff trauma for hours after. We had one of those bad days in February 1970 when the Vice President faced his first serious crisis—the Bob Hope Desert Classic in Palm Springs.

Bob had, by this time, developed a solid friendship with Spiro and convinced him that his presence at the Hope Classic would be a big draw for the Eisenhower Medical Center, the financial recipient of the Classic's profits. As we drove in the limousine through throngs of golfing fans toward the first hole at Bermuda Dunes Country Club, Agnew was tense and white. I'm sure he would rather have taken his chances on the University of California's Berkeley campus than face that first tee. Fans lined the entire fairway, TV cameras were everywhere, and the crowd responded enthusiastically to the tall man with silver-gray hair, blue slacks, and a white Izod shirt.

"Well, Peter, here goes my image . . . right out of bounds!"

Awaiting his arrival, Hope tickled the crowd as he bantered with the rest of the foursome—professional golfer Doug Sanders and baseball's Willie Mays. Sanders was introduced first and, from the back tee, whacked one down the middle three hundred yards. Hope was up next and, tossing off a couple of classic lines, hit the ball a respectable two hundred twenty yards to the right center of the fairway.

"And now, ladies and gentlemen," the public-address system blared, "the Vice President of the United States, Spiro T. Agnew." Big applause. The clicking of cameras sounded like a horde of locusts. I turned to Art Sohmer and, in silence, we hid our eyes. The silence was broken by a chorus of "Oh's!" "Ah's!" and "Oh, my God's!"

Our worst fears had materialized. Somewhere about thirty yards down the narrow alley of bright shirts and sunburned faces, Agnew's ball had found its mark—the head of a spectator.

Absolutely beside himself, Agnew dashed to his unintended victim and, after being reassured that no serious damage had been inflicted, returned to the first tee and hit the safest shot possible—a topped wood, fifty yards down the middle. The working press had already broken for the phones and no attention was paid to Willie Mays, who drilled a second victim on a line drive two hundred fifty yards down the left side of the fairway.

Despite his awesome start, Agnew kept cool and, given a wider fairway, finished the round without further disaster. He was, however, to live with that golf rap for the rest of the year. No one let him forget it, and he never let me forget that it was *my* suggestion that he play.

Later that month, Agnew returned to the Springs, this time as the guest of Irish-American multimillionaire Jack Mulcahey. Mulcahey had been a generous contributor to the Nixon-Agnew campaign and a good friend of the President's. Nixon aide Henry Cashen admired Agnew a great deal and suggested Agnew cultivate Mulcahey's friendship. Jack had two beautiful homes at Thunderbird Country Club near Palm Springs and graciously offered both to the Veep and his staff. While we were guests at his home, I received a call through the White House switchboard from one of Elvis Presley's aides. Elvis, it seemed, was also a fan of Agnew's and wanted to meet and spend a little time with him. The aide mentioned that Mr. Presley had a gift for Agnew as well and wanted to present it personally to him. I was curious. What does Elvis really want? I thought. There's got to be a political angle here somewhere.

Spiro T. found the situation amusing. But also curious as to what Elvis could have in mind, he said, "Sure. Go ahead. Invite him over for cocktails."

Elvis himself called me back to check on the time and whether or not the dress was to be typically Palm Springs casual.

They came over that evening for cocktails. I say "they" because Elvis arrived with an entourage. What we on Agnew's staff found interesting about the retinue was that it was an identical setup to that which was provided to the Vice President by the Secret Service. Gun-for-gun and man-for-man, they matched our protective barricade. The automobiles arrived, and one of the Secret Service agents (Chuck Vance, who later married Susan Ford) pulled me aside, saying with a grin, "Peter, we've got a little problem here. This group is as well armed as we are, right down to Uzi machine guns. You know that puts a burden on us, because armed men just don't visit with the Vice President."

Elvis himself was not carrying a gun, but his top aide was. The Vice President had not yet appeared. Never having met Presley before, I was in an awkward situation. But he was pleasant and instantly accommodating when I called him aside. Laughingly, he said, "Wait 'til you see my gift."

Presley was good-natured, very articulate, and much more right-wing than I would have gathered from his public image. He was dressed in a conservative suit with an open-collared shirt, a very simple gold chain, and an ordinary wedding band—hardly the sequined rock 'n' roll star we all expected. I had never really thought about Presley in a political context, but he seemed deeply concerned about the affairs of his country and Mr. Agnew's stand on them. His chat with the Vice President was warm and leaned toward serious discussions about the government's direction. He asked Agnew some very penetrating questions on foreign policy, especially about Vietnam. It wasn't the typical celebrity-to-Veep chitchat that so often arises in similar social settings.

Agnew told me later that Presley was trying to get a better grasp of the problems facing the country and had offered his services wherever Agnew thought he could best help. Presley also wanted to visit Washington and talk to the President, and Agnew agreed to make the arrangements.

Before he left, Elvis presented the Vice President with two magnificent, pearl-handled six-shooters with ivory inlay. They were later appraised at over $5,000, which exceeded the legal gift limitation, and were therefore returned with a grateful note. (The Vice President was allowed to accept valuable gifts only if they were given by a head of state, and even then they became the automatic property of the State Department.) After Elvis left, Agnew remarked how impressed he was with him and how he wished more stars with such broad appeal would take on the interest that Elvis had.

In September, I heard through Dinah Shore that Frank Sinatra also admired the Vice President and respected him for being so forthright in his views. Agnew had met Dinah the year before through C. D. Ward, a bright Agnew aide and a good tennis player. Agnew often played tennis with Dinah and her handsome clan at her home in Beverly Hills, and Dinah became a good friend to both Spiro and Judy. In fact, one evening over cocktails, she even lured him into a rare talk-show guest spot. Since he normally despised programs of that nature, his acceptance was a tribute to their friendship and Dinah's considerable charm.

I had known Sinatra since my childhood in Toluca Lake where his home, then, was only a few blocks from both the Hopes' and the Malatestas'. We certainly weren't pals, but my name and face were familiar to him. In October, I mentioned to Agnew Sinatra's interest. Agnew was surprised and somewhat flattered, and he told me to talk it over with Art Sohmer and Roy Goodearle, his senior political adviser. These two gentlemen had mixed feelings about such an alliance, but they voiced only minor concern and left the bottom line to Agnew and myself. It made sense to me. Sinatra was one of the most charismatic and exciting performers in decades. I knew him to be a great host and a most generous person, and, though he had always been politically identified with the Democrats, particularly during the Kennedy years, I thought, why not? Let's introduce him to our man. Who knows where it might lead?

Frank Sinatra had always intrigued me. As a P.R. man, I never could understand his inconsistent public image, ranging from philanthropist to rascal. His many friends literally adored him but few could ever be specific as to just why. I wanted to know this living legend myself. What was he really all about? On our next trip to Palm Springs, I *would* arrange that meeting.

Following the off-year congressional campaign of 1970, Agnew invited me to join him as his guest on a trip to Hawaii. The staff worked hard and this jaunt was to be a reward. I was not on the payroll yet, but I felt the time was close. I resigned from my consultant position with the oil firm; I, too, welcomed the vacation. We booked into the Khahali Hilton Hotel for four days of real R and R. As things turned out, we got more rest than the Secret Service did.

As steadfast as the Secret Service is, this particular trip to Hawaii put those guys in a genuine panic over an incident involving the Vice President and a frisky teenager. Our group was lounging by the lagoon off the deck of the Khahali, and, as usual, full protection for the Vice President was present. When the man goes swimming, the Secret Service swim with him.

A boy who ran the equipment concession there took advantage of a very windy day to sail on one of his catamarans. This kid had earlier invited the Vice President for a ride, but the invitation was pooh-poohed by the Secret Service and the young man went off on his own. Agnew was swimming with Mary Ellen Warner, his secretary, and myself (and the S.S., of course), when our young sailor breezed by in his catamaran. He made a beautiful tack in the wind and slid in front of Agnew, saying, "Hello, Mr. Vice President! Would you like a ride?!"

Not knowing the kid already had been refused permission, Spiro was delighted. "I've never been on one of those things before," he chirped. "I'd love a ride!" He hopped on, pulling Mary Ellen with him, and shouted, "C'mon, Peter!" but by then the kid again tacked and they were flying off, making a big curve in the lagoon.

You have never seen such commotion from the Secret Service. At present, their primary purpose in life was to guard the man who had just sailed away. As I crawled out of the water, all the radio equipment was squawking full blast. I said to agent Sam Sulliman, "Wouldn't it be funny if that boy is some spy and right outside the reef is a Russian submarine waiting to surface and whisk old Ted-Baby back to Moscow?" Sam has a good sense of humor, but somehow this didn't strike him as funny at all.

By this time, the catamaran was a good two hundred yards out and heading toward the open sea. "There he goes—Spiro Who?—off into the sunset!" I yelled to Sam. I was visually drilled by a deep, .38 caliber stare for my trouble.

Within thirty seconds, a Coast Guard boat and a helicopter were converging on the catamaran. Meanwhile, the kid made a well-executed 180° turn and smoothly steered Agnew back into the lagoon. It was a nice, five-minute ride.

The Secret Service said nothing to Agnew but pulled the youngster aside and gave him a good bawling out. That subsequently got him fired from the hotel. I went down the next day to straighten things out. The young sport may have done something wrong, but he didn't deserve to be sacked. Agnew supported my action, having enjoyed his spontaneous ride and not wanting to see his captain canned. The Secret Service agreed not to press charges and the hotel relented as well.

On the return flight from Hawaii, I reminded Agnew of Dinah Shore's remark concerning Sinatra's interest. We were going into Los Angeles that night and then down to Palm Springs for a week. This seemed to be as good a time as any to bring the two men together.

Agnew approved and suggested I try to add Frank to our foursome during our forthcoming stay. I shuddered and blurted out, "Geeze, sir, I want you to meet the guy, not kill him."

I called Frank's home, and he promptly returned my call. Agnew and I already had a golf game scheduled with Bob Hope, and I asked Frank if he would like to join us. He said he would like to meet Vice President Agnew but that recent hand surgery prevented him from playing golf at this time. He said he'd grab a cart and join us on the second nine to kibbitz.

The spark of friendship between Agnew and Sinatra ignited on the first take. We had one hell of an afternoon, as you could have only with Hope and Sinatra at their leisurely best. The wisecracks flew better than the golf balls. The weather was perfect, and so was the collective ambiance. Over postgame cocktails, Frank invited the Vice President to visit his compound the next day. He explained that he had to return to Los Angeles but assured us that Nancy Sinatra, Sr., would be delighted to show us around. Agnew accepted with pleasure. As scheduled, he, Judy, and I made our first visit to the desert world of Frank Sinatra.

Although long ago divorced, Frank and Nancy were still very good friends, and even though we were newcomers it wasn't difficult to observe that a lot of love lingered between them. Nancy was to be, on several occasions, hostess and party planner at the compound. She totally complemented Frank's sense of style and understood the kind of ambiance he wanted his home to exude.

Judy and Nancy's rapport was as instant as Frank and Spiro's. We had a lush afternoon. I knew we'd be back!

The following month, on December 27, 1970, Agnew returned to Palm Springs, and I arranged for us to guest at the grand home of my friends George and Rosalie Hearst. After a small and quiet dinner at Don the Beachcomber's, we returned to the Hearst house. The Vice President called me aside for a private meeting. It was at this time that I was officially asked to join his staff as special assistant to the Vice President and senior traveling aide. I could hardly contain myself and I blurted out, "I thought you'd never ask!"

Nevertheless, I thought it was time to be candid with my new boss regarding my attitude toward the President. Agnew listened with tight attention as I related my grievances toward Richard Nixon. I really never liked R.N., even when I liked him! All through the years of my dealings with Nixon, I always had the feeling that he had a phony way of handling people. I've seen him treat supporters as if they were the best thing since metal tips on shoelaces, and the next moment, after their departure, tell an aide, "Don't ever bring that son-of-a-bitch around again."

His talent for managing complicated affairs on an international scale bordered on genius; his political backroom astuteness had Machiavellian brilliance; but his inability to cope honestly with day-to-day life is now legend. The only thing consistent about that was inconsistency.

In 1961, after his defeat by JFK, he returned to California depressed and awkward. Pat and the girls remained in Washington and a lonely R.N. arrived *sans* aides, press, and limos. My good friend Jim Golden, a former secret service agent, advanced Nixon's arrival and tried in vain to find suitable but reasonable accommodations for the former Vice President.

After a "Can you help?" call from Jim, I talked to Jack Haley, Sr., a good Republican and a confidant to all his son's friends. Mr. Haley was never too busy to return anyone's calls and mine was no exception. I explained R.N.'s dilemma, and he promptly assured me that although he had no openings in any of his many properties, he'd find something "for our good V.P." Two days later, Haley called back and said he made arrangements with a good friend of his who owned the Gaylord Hotel for a complimentary suite for Mr. Nixon, for as long as he wanted to stay.

Golden asked me if I'd stay around for a while and help out until Nixon's family and staff arrived. I agreed, and Haley quickly arranged another complimentary suite for us. During the short time I was an aide, I found Nixon to be interesting, sullen, and complicated. I dined with him a number of times and often no conversation would be exchanged—literally not a word. I could tell he was seriously depressed and morosely introspective. These first few months after his defeat seemed particularly painful, and I tried my best to cheer him up, but he rarely responded.

The one consolation he enjoyed was long drives up and down the Pacific coast highway. One Sunday, as we piled into his big, four-door lavender Oldsmobile, I suggested we drive up to the Hope home and have a visit with Bob. Nixon had been shrouded in gloom for weeks, and I thought if anybody could cheer him up, it would be Hope.

We drove to Toluca Lake, rang at the big gates, and entered the house.

Bob was upstairs in bed, watching a football game on television. I went into his room and greeted him, saying, "I think I may have done something a little presumptuous." Hope shot me one of those "What now!?" glances. "Richard Nixon's downstairs," I blurted, "and he's really in the dumps!" Hope was taken aback: "Dick's here?! . . . Tell him I'll be right down."

Although I ruined his quiet Sunday, Hope responded graciously. He was up and dressed and cracking jokes before he got to the bottom of the stairs. An afternoon with Hope can do wonders, even for a wounded political warrior. While they visited privately and hit golf balls and such, I took in the rest of the ball game so I could at least tell Bob the score. When we returned to the Gaylord Hotel that evening, Nixon was in a bright, talkative mood, saying that the visit had been a real turning point for him.

Later that month, there was much speculation that Nixon might run for governor of California against incumbent Pat Brown. I was picking up on the rumors but remained silent, feeling that, in time, Nixon would either tell me or he wouldn't. At the peak of this brouhaha, he and I sat down to dinner one night and he asked me, "Peter, what do you think my chances are for the governorship of California?"

I was floored by the thought of it because I couldn't understand how a man who missed the presidency by an eyelash would want to settle now, so soon after, for a state position. The best plan seemed to me to be that he should practice law, stay in the international scene, and groom his platform for the 1964 race.

So I told him I didn't like the sound of it, right off the bat. He had everything to lose and nothing to gain. By staying a private citizen, accepting speaking engagements both abroad and at home, and by just being a former Vice President, he'd have himself perfectly positioned for another run at the presidency. I could not see how, under those circumstances, the party could possibly deny him the nomination.

I told him that Pat Brown was no pushover; he was an articulate, friendly governor in a state that was, even at that time, heavily Democratic. The odds were against Nixon, and it was just too soon after a major defeat. I said I didn't want him to look as though he needed a job that badly.

He nodded approvingly and told me it was sage advice with

which he agreed. Feeling bright and politically astute for my age, I went home that night confident that I might have contributed something significant to a man whom I felt was probably going to be President someday.

The next week, I attended a dinner party with some high-ranking state Republicans who told me I didn't know what I was talking about! Nixon was going to announce his gubernatorial candidacy in a few days, they said, and he had already made up his mind the day before I had dinner with him.

"No way!" I said. "He told me last week that he wasn't going to run. We had a wonderful talk and I know he wouldn't mislead me. You're wrong!"

Bullshit! Twenty-four hours later he announced his candidacy. I wished him the best of luck and severed myself from him and his organization. I was more idealistic then and couldn't believe that a guy like this would sit down and boldface lead me on, pick my brain, and tell me what a sharp politician I was, and then turn around and do just the opposite of what he said he'd do. I was almost pleased when he lost to Pat Brown!

After that, I lost touch with him, seeing him only once briefly on the campaign trail for Barry Goldwater in 1964. Maybe, in retrospect, it was petty of me to have become so incensed over what merely amounted to political double-talk. But although the substance of our conversation that night had been political, the context was personal, and for that reason I took his subsequent behavior personally. I no longer liked or trusted Richard Nixon and I wanted Agnew to know it.

Thoughtfully, the Vice President commented that I was entitled to my opinion and that he would do nothing to dissuade me. But he reminded me that he had been chosen by, and worked for, Richard Nixon. He would demand at least professional respect for the President from all his staff members, and I was to be no exception. Henceforth, I would keep my opinions of R.N. to myself. I agreed—for the time, anyway.

He shook my hand and asked if I was prepared to return to Washington with him on the third of January. I said I was. Then we both turned in, Agnew to sleep and me to brief the rest of the staff who already had a bottle of champagne popped in celebration.

The final two days of 1970 were packed with excitement for me. We had dinner at Sinatra's on the thirtieth and helicoptered up to

Hope's New Hollywood estate for for their New Year's Eve party. Dr. Bill Voss, by now a good friend of mine, gave me a diuretic pill a half-hour before the chopper took off, as I had been celebrating my new job with considerable liquid intake and felt bloated. About twenty minutes out of Palm Springs, my bladder responded with overwhelming pressure. I had forgotten that I was not flying in the vice-presidential helicopter, with its private head. Instead, we were aboard a Marine Corps chopper out of El Toro and it had no private relief accommodations. Good God, I thought. No wonder the Marines are so fierce, they don't pee! I grew paler. No place in the manual of a V.P. aide is a predicament like this covered. My two-day-old job foiled because of a lack of a john!

Good mother that she is, Mrs. Agnew was aware of the problem of the newest staff member and kept teasing me, which, of course, helped naught; the last thing I wanted to do was laugh. She turned to her husband and said, "Spiro, Peter has to go to the bathroom!"

Agnew was detached. "What do you want me to do about it?"

I blurted out, "The *least* you could do, *Mister* Vice President, is land at the next gas station!"

He laughed, but thoughtfully checked out that possibility with the pilot. I reneged and offered to use the relief tube in the rear of the helicopter if everyone would shut their eyes . . . and ears. More laughs for them, but what a relief for me!

Although that New Year's Eve at the Hopes was just family and good friends, it was memorable for me. Most of Bob's relatives from Cleveland were present, as well as Dolores' family, my dear Grandmother Theresa, Mother and Dad, and my brother Tom. Old friends like Flo and Jerry Colonna, Johnny and Ginger Mercer, Toots Shor, George Shearing, Senator and Mrs. Stu Symington, the Bob Stantons, and Les and Claire Brown joined the newcomer Agnews in wishing each other a happy 1971, and in wishing me luck in my new appointment.

Four days later, I was ensconced in my new office in the old Executive Office Building, a mere chip shot from the Rose Garden. I pinched myself. In less than twenty-four months, I had achieved a unique goal: I was where I wanted to be. For the first time in my life, I was looking no further.

23

We spent nine days in D.C. Little did I realize that the next time I would have the luxury of nine consecutive days in my new home was seven months down the road. For the next thirty-three months, we would travel to all fifty states, over one hundred cities, and around the world twice. I would see power rise and crash, friendships bloom and wither, and the history of the country altered beyond comprehension.

Chapter Two

After the swearing in of the Ninety-second Congress, we flew to Houston, Texas, for the first annual Vince Lombardi Award Dinner and my first official trip as a traveling aide. We stayed at the AstroWorld Hotel in what was known as the Celestial Suite. I've stayed in fine hotels all over the world, but this layout is the living end! Each of the rooms rivals the set design of *Hello, Dolly!* The master suite had a black porcelain, S-shaped, fifteen-foot tub in the bathroom. At the end of the hall was a private double-decker discotheque and bar complete with piano, billiard table, and pinball machines.

After spending an hour or so in our private disco, Spiro seemed to be enjoying himself. He had a couple of Chivas Regals with soda and engaged in one lighthearted conversation after another. While this gathering went on, several thousand people were entering the Grand Ballroom for the evening's program. I was like the proverbial cat on a hot tin roof—checking out the podium for height; the lighting; a double check with the press secretary; a walk through the proposed route; a quick check-through of Agnew's speech for proper order. I was a wreck!

Meanwhile, the rest of the staff awaited my return in our private Shangri-la. As I entered the disco to announce that all was ready, Spiro suddenly faltered off his barstool. He didn't fall, but he weaved noticeably, saying, "My God, something's wrong. Peter, you know how it is—every once in a while when you travel you have a couple of drinks and they hit you wrong."

He faltered again and his arm slipped off the bar. I panicked. Could it be? The Vice President was bombed!

He said, "Peter, dear friend . . ." (something *was* wrong—he *never* called me "dear friend") "When you have a few drinks and you're traveling and you're tired, they can hit you differently than usual. Please stall them downstairs. I'm too tight right now to speak."

At that precise moment, our advance man signalled me on the walkie-talkie that the head table was in place. Mrs. Lombardi, Senator Tower, the mayor, and everyone else had been seated. I could "bring the man down any time."

I turned to Agnew. "Sir, I'm sure you can do it if you try."

"No, no. I feel a little high. Too high to go down there and do that. Go tell 'em something, Peter. Tell 'em I'm going to take a nap, but I'll be down in an hour and a half. I just need a little nap."

I said, "Sir, did you really say *'an hour and a half'*?"

"Tell them I need a nap!" He was raising his voice. "I'm a little tired. But if they stand by, I'll be down as soon as I wake up."

I was close to panic. *I* was the one responsible for conveying the message to thousands of patiently waiting people that the Vice President of the United States was too tipsy to speak. The 1972 campaign was not that far away. John Connally was in the wings. We had the momentum going our way, but this was not time for my man to blow a big speech. I saw every paper in the country jumping on this story.

I started searching frantically for a good lie. No way was I going to explain how bombed he was. If he needed an hour and a half, I had to come up with a quickly cured illness or a stuck elevator—something. I had to think of something! As I pressed the elevator button, I heard a strong, clear vice-presidential voice say, "Pete . . . Peter . . . relax!"

There was the Vice President, sober as a potato, and I had witnessed a performance worthy of an Emmy. He had just wanted to see how I'd handle it. How I *would* have handled it I still don't know, but I can tell you one thing: You can talk about your Atkins diet, your Scarsdale diet, your high protein diet, but I can guarantee that I lost thirteen pounds from the time I saw he wasn't riding his barstool right to the time I pressed the elevator button.

Southern California's jolting earthquake in February 1971 brought the Vice President to Van Nuys for a view of the disaster area and a recommendation for federal aid. Coincidentally, the Bob Hope

Desert Classic of 1971 was the same week. I wondered whether Van Nuys might be an omen of things to come.

We arrived at Palm Springs Airport in the afternoon and motorcaded to the home of the Leonard Firestones at Thunderbird Country Club. The next four days were filled with activities. There was always something to keep everyone occupied. The Agnew kids, Randy and Kim, swam, sunned, and explored the desert. Mrs. A. shopped and enjoyed her new Palm Springs friends. Agnew prepped for his appearance later that week in the golf tournament, and I spent my free time lounging at Sinatra's.

On the night before the classic we all went to the Hopes' for their traditional pre-tournament Italian dinner. Of all the annual parties I've attended, year after year this one is consistently the best. Most of the golfers participating in the Classic and their wives, along with the playing celebrities, attend. It's always been obvious to me that this party is the Hopes' favorite get-together.

The following day was Lincoln's birthday, and all our gang went to Danny Schwartz's for dinner. Danny was a good friend and business associate of Frank's, and he and his wife, Natalie, entertained us royally in their beautiful home adjacent to Tamarisk Country Club. Cocktails were served at the appointed hour, but Sinatra was nowhere to be seen. A bit unusual for Frank, because he is a remarkably punctual man. As cocktail hour peaked, in walked this figure in a stovepipe hat, a full set of whiskers, and a black shawl. The figure spoke: "Four scored and a few didn't."

We were still laughing at "Abe" Sinatra's schtick when the lead Secret Service agent called me aside and informed me politely that Danny Thomas had a gun tucked in his pants.

Jesus! I thought. First Presley, now Thomas! What's with these actors?

Danny and Rosemary Thomas have been friends of mine for more years than I care to remember, and there certainly wasn't any warranted concern for the Vice President's safety. But, once again, I was put in the awkward situation of having a guest disarmed. I discreetly mentioned it to Frank, who said he'd handle the situation, adding, "I've seen Danny's act. It's too late for him to be scared."

Danny and Spiro hit it off well. For every moment of Thomas' humor, there is a balancing side of serious purpose. Danny's dedication to his favorite charities—particularly St. Jude's Hospital—is ever-present. Through the next few years, Danny would use Agnew to further these worthwhile causes. Spiro, in turn, would use Thomas to bolster his crushed credentials after his resignation. It was Thomas who flew in from the West Coast to lend his presence and support at a reception of Arab ambassadors with whom Agnew wanted to curry favor. Indeed, one hand washed the other.

For the second straight year, Agnew did it again! The Vice President of the United States beaned another voter at the Hope Classic!

God! I thought, I hope it was a Democrat; we can't afford to lose any more Republicans!

Fortunately, an ice cube was all the medicine needed, and Spiro resorted once more to his tried-and-true topped bunt down the middle of the fairway.

One thing I did notice about Agnew and his golf game was that weekend golfers related to Agnew's anguish over his game. The precise pros who did it for a living are a vision of near-perfect motion, but let's face it, most golfers are hackers and they loved Agnew's spunk for even showing up.

I had the good fortune during the tournament to have double accommodations. Agnew's traveling staff was provided with rooms at Canyon Country Club, but I was also a guest at the Firestones. Naturally, I stayed close to the Agnews, but I used the country club facilities, too. It was there that I ran into an old pal, a West Coast socialite who still looked like the gorgeous green-eyed beauty at least one president couldn't forget. I invited her to dinner at Sinatra's that night as my date, and later, after we had driven back to the club, we began to pick up the threads of our old romance.

She said, "This is really a pleasant surprise, Peter."

"Why?" I asked. (I didn't care, but one must be polite.)

"Through the years," she explained, "you'd pay attention to me and then you wouldn't. You'd look at me and then you'd look at other girls, and I thought, frankly, you were an insincere flirt. I never knew where you were at."

"Well," I purred, "let's have some fun and talk about sincerity tomorrow."

And indeed we did enjoy ourselves. We frolicked quite playfully for an hour or so, but I could see myself losing some ground. The weekend's hectic pace and Frank's wine were elements working against me.

At this point, I'll have to digress briefly to explain that Agnew's personal physician, Dr. Bill Voss, was a very accommodating fellow who automatically offered his services to any member of the staff with a physical problem. He pampered us, and it got to the point that one ran to him with the slightest little thing that one would normally never need a doctor for. I, being a newcomer, was not used to the pace of the traveling staff, and good Doctor Bill would administer vitamin B-12 shots which always gave me a quick recharge.

Now, in the dawn's early light, I began to think I needed Bill's help. My beautiful friend had just made an offer I couldn't refuse—or, at any rate, damn well wasn't going to refuse if I could help it. So I dialed Bill with one arm, the other being occupied. "Bill, could you discreetly come into my room, because I'm losing my attention span, so to speak, and could you bring a booster shot of B-12? But please, not too much dialogue, because I've got some company."

My friend started to laugh, then demurely ducked her head under the covers.

A moment later, Dr. Voss crept into the room, his slippers flapping and syringe in hand. He pulled the sheet down, stuck me in the butt with the needle, patted me on the puncture, said "Carry on," and serenely paddled out again. I thought I'd never get that damn woman to stop laughing.

In late February, Sinatra made his first trip to Washington as an Agnew pal, and this arrival seemed a perfect time for me to make my entry into the social world of the Capital. With Frank as guest of honor and the Agnews as frosting, I still had no idea who would turn out for Peter Malatesta's first "cake," but I would give it a try. As I still lived in temporary quarters, I chose Taloe House for the occasion. Taloe is just around the corner from the White House, in a row of historic buildings available to high-ranking officials for just such receptions.

This was to be my first real opportunity to gather social and media attention as a host. Besides just wanting to have a good party to reciprocate for Frank's desert hospitality, I wanted to cultivate my public identity in Washington as being far more than just another Agnew aide. I knew Sinatra would draw guests like moths to a klieg light, and I also knew no one in the administration was ready to stick his or her neck out and go on record as hosting and toasting the controversial entertainer. I anticipated some flack from the Oval Office but, hell, I thought, I'm ready for a social debut and 1600 Pennsylvania *will* get over it.

I was very pleased with the turnout. Several members of the presidential cabinet and their wives, including John and Martha Mitchell, attended. Governors Ron Reagan, Richard Ogilvie of Illinois, Arch Moore of West Virginia, and Edgar Whitcomb of Indiana dropped by on their way to a governors' reception across the street. Congressman Barry Goldwater of California, astronaut Alan Shepard, and many more all came to give Frank a warm welcome to Washington.

It snowed heavily that night and I was concerned about Sinatra's arrival by private jet. My concern turned to worry as I heard both Washington's National and Dulles airports had closed. My first big shindig and no guest of honor! My fear passed with the arrival of Frank—an hour late, but no one cared. He was quick to tell the story of how they were forced to land in Baltimore after he told the pilot, "Forget the snow. Just bring this baby down to the nearest limo. I've got people waiting!"

My first big party was an eye-opener. It amazed me how easily accessible the city's uppercrust actually was, once a "trump card" like Sinatra was played. As guest of honor, he drew a crowd that a hosting newcomer like myself would presuppose to be impossible. Just as glittery Hollywood was agog over the appearance of an Agnew, Goldwater, or Kennedy, Washington society proved that it would turn out in droves if a host or hostess could produce a fantasy-object like Frank Sinatra.

But Washington differs from Los Angeles in one important aspect. Washington is highly compact, with "biggies" practically living on top of one another within a relatively small city. Gossip can spread like wildfire because of this closeness, and a host with a "big gun" can get the town's seemingly undivided attention—for one night anyway. The Los Angeles that I knew, on the other hand, was a spread-out and disenfranchised collection of small cities. Hollywood, for example, neither mingled with nor cared about the social cliques in Palos Verdes. In Washington, everyone was in the same basket by virtue of proximity, while in L.A. one had to choose from fifty baskets. I realized as I assessed the success of my first party that I had the

Hollywood connections to keep the party trump cards coming. Who knew where it all might lead?

The Gridiron Club in Washington hosts a yearly dinner attended by the most prominent members of the national press and the most prestigious political and military figures in the Capital. This year, the event fell in March. The program consists of short speeches and, of course, many gags and skits. It's always a very amusing, very elegant night.

In 1971, Spiro Agnew attended at Nixon's request. (Presidents are always invited and, through the years, many have attended.) The "big gun" Democrat that year was Ted Kennedy.

After beaning people with golf balls for two years running, we knew Agnew was going to take his share of knocks. It was also a year in which Mr. Agnew had had a little trouble with his press relations. One particular network had gotten under his skin a bit and he, in his usual candid manner, had from time to time "let 'em have it."

Agnew wanted the best material possible. We knew that Senator Kennedy would be equipped with his usual quick wit (Teddy's a tough act to follow), so Bob Hope turned his top gag writers loose, and Paul Keyes, the genius behind TV's "Laugh-In," also contributed. Thus, Agnew was at his (Hope's) best.

But the topper of the evening was yet to come. Victor Gold, the Vice President's clever and talented press secretary, and I had an idea. While Agnew was speaking, I was to crawl behind the podium with a six-foot wooden bow and a leather sack of arrows, and Vic was to unfurl a huge picture of the CBS "eye" at the right moment. I was no stranger to the Secret Service, so when I started snaking on my hands and knees behind the podium with my big bow, the agents looked on with indifference. But the others on the platform were not so inclined. They didn't know me from Adam. There were several Supreme Court justices, John Connally, Ted Kennedy, Elliot Richardson, Alf Landon, Richard Helms, Gerald Ford, Carl Albert, Maurice Stans, and George Romney, among others. And here comes the "assassin" crawling behind them on his knees in black tie with a reasonably obvious weapon. Everybody had one nervous eye over his shoulder as I moved along. I cracked up. Each glance had a cautious, "Well, I guess it's okay" air to it. Of course, it couldn't possibly be an assassination. But if it were, what nerve! And if it is, who's going to get it? On a tight podium from a distance of two feet? But nobody said a word, because that's Washington. They apparently thought that, in my own way, I must have belonged there. Nevertheless, one out of every two eyes on that platform was glued in the opposite direction.

I reached Spiro's feet on cue, just as he was saying to the audience that he was giving up golf once and for all and had selected a marvelous new sport. I popped up with my bundle of arrows; Spiro took the bow and pulled heartily as Vic unravelled the target. Big howl! Relieved podium! Typical gridiron!

Fortunately, Agnew did not shoot the arrow. That's all we would have needed!

In early April Agnew delivered a speech in Los Angeles before the Chamber of Commerce, and we again made the 26-minute flight to Palm Springs. Although we had by now spent much time at Sinatra's, this was our first trip as house guests. The Vice President's growing friendship with Frank had come under some petty criticism from the White House and from inside his own staff. I always suspected jealousy as the motive, but Agnew passed it off with an impervious shrug. Frank's compound was an ideal setup for Agnew. Security was almost perfect, and the facilities rivaled the best resorts. But, most of all, it gave us a chance to enjoy life with Sinatra.

Chapter Three

Life With Sinatra. Three simple words—hiding behind them is a private world so full of excitement, luxury, and warmth that it is utterly mind-boggling. And the nucleus of this world is his compound in Palm Springs.

It is the most perfect setup for entertaining guests that I have ever seen. Every detail in the physical plant has Frank's special touch. Everything has its place and everyone who works for Frank knows his job. The compound is adjacent to Tamarisk Country Club, off the eighth fairway. It started out with just one house but kept on growing. Now the compound, surrounded by oleanders hiding an electric fence, consists of the main house and three smaller guest quarters that are self-contained homes. There is a heliport, tennis court, swimming pool, a railroad car converted to a health club, and the "Christmas tree" house, which is a separate four-bedroom home on the rear of Frank's property.

Every bedroom in the compound has two bathrooms, and even the medicine cabinets in each of these many bathrooms are perfectly stocked. Closets waiting for each guest have new slippers and new bathrobes. The compound contains a full, professional kitchen with 24-hour service by hotline from every room. Each guest suite has its own Pullman kitchen, fully stocked, so if you prefer a morning or evening of privacy, you can stay in your new bathrobe and have a snack.

Frank's perfectionist attitude extends deeply into his sense of being a host. And there he shines the brightest. He anticipates the needs of his guests before they arise. Sinatra painstakingly schedules his myriad guests with a perfect concern toward their compatibility. Regulars at his home during the Agnew days included Barbara Marx, daughters Tina and Nancy, the Ronald Reagans, Roz Russell and Freddie Brisson, Jimmy Van Heusen, former New York City mayor Robert Wagner, the Milton Berles, Dr. Michael De Bakey, the Bennett Cerfs, and at least on one occasion Grace and Rainier of Monaco and their family.

The program of the day was full but flexible. You got up when you wanted to, although mid-morning golf rounds were the usual. Tee-off was seldom before 11:00 A.M. Breakfast was a matter of wandering into the dining room and ordering whatever you wanted. To be sure, the morning feast was never the best-attended meal; only the golfers would eat heartily before fighting the traps. The one person you could always count on seeing at the breakfast table was Frank, peering over his Ben Franklin glasses, working in ink on *The New York Times* crossword puzzle, and sipping coffee.

Golf was the main activity until the early afternoon. Lunch by the pool varied from the old-fashioned New York hot dog cart to a fresh-fruit buffet. Mid-afternoon was devoted to tennis, and often a fresh batch of friends, the likes of Dinah Shore, Danny Schwartz, and Rod Laver, would come over for a few hours and swing a racket. If anyone were caught short of tennis gear, he or she could, of course, go to the compound storeroom and choose a new outfit from shorts to tennis shoes.

At five or five-thirty, all gathered in the main bar for cocktails and small talk. It was the perfect time to pull out a new joke or rib Frank for a bad putt. Almost no business was ever discussed *then.* It was a time to relax.

From six to about nine o'clock, you were on your own—to nap, read, have a massage, or whatever. The household gathered again after 8:30 for pre-dinner cocktails. The dress was comfortable—sport jacket or sweater, California slacks, and an open-collared shirt.

The dining room was set in beautiful, candlelit round tables of six, and hung with paintings by Monet, Pissarro, Boudin, and Utrillo. Often Frank or his mother, Dolly, would do the cooking, especially if the fare was to be Italian. Momma Sinatra usually made the sauce, although Frank was equally skilled as an Italian chef and particularly noteworthy for his chicken, Italian-style. The house wine is usually Chateau Lafite Rothschild, decanted. Frank's not fussy—he's quite content with the best.

After-dinner toasts always concluded a great meal. These might range from Milton Berle's nonsense to something serious from the Vice President to a warm and graceful flourish from Prince Rainier. Then, perhaps, Lenny Haiten would excite the Bosendorfer concert grand piano and we'd all relax in the company of Frank and look at his collection of Fabergé boxes or other objects. Coffee would be served and, with that, we'd move into the theater—a long, lounging room with a bar, fireplace, and pool table. Nightly films of a current box-office hit, a still-unreleased picture, or a glorious old classic were next on the program. Naturally, after a Sinatra meal, there were always a few dozers. Sometimes the only three left by the end of the evening would be Frank, Barbara, and myself. If the movie was dull, Frank would have it shut off and start a game of pool, at which he and Agnew excelled.

Toward the end of the evening, the stragglers would head back to the main bar for a nightcap and some small talk before retiring. By then, it was stag time, and the mood varied. There were bourbon nights, Stolichnaya nights, wine nights. Frank has a graceful way of sliding out when he's tired—no formal farewells, just a simple *ciao* or a wave of the hand. His low-keyed exit never gave one the feeling that the party was over.

My favorite late moments were spent alone after everyone had turned in. I'd stretch out on the couch by the fireplace in the theater and listen to the sounds of Tony Bennett, Ella Fitzgerald, or Count Basie. If you couldn't see them in person, the next best thing was listening to them on Frank's flawless Quadrophonic system in a specially designed room.

For all the stories that are told dealing with Frank's discipline, or lack of it, he has the most extraordinary sense of personal order. He can move at a gazelle pace or drag his heels like a stubborn burro. But either way is by his calculated choice. When he's booked for a recording session or a concert series, his self-discipline is almost military.

One story that amuses those who understand Frank's sense of perfection goes like this: He rose one morning, looked at the pool, six or seven feet beyond the glass doors of his bedroom, and decided it was too close for safety. He called in his head honcho and told him to move the pool fifteen feet and to have it done that week, if possible.

The following month, we flew to Austin, Texas, for the dedication of the LBJ Library. Aboard Air Force Two were an assortment of congressional dignitaries and several members of the Supreme Court. The Vice President called me into his compartment and told me he wanted to dispense with protocol when we got off the plane in Austin. It was customary for only the President or Veep to exit from the front of the aircraft; all guests and staff left from the rear door. As a gesture of courtesy, Agnew instructed me to advise our distinguished guests that he would like them to disembark from the front door.

It was no national secret that Agnew had qualms about some of the opinions rendered by the Supreme Court, especially by some of the more liberal members. One of our guests happened to be Justice Thurgood Marshall, a bulwark of liberalism. Although Agnew had never met Marshall, he was predisposed not to like him. Staff members Roy Goodearle and David Keene were very sensitive to Agnew's prejudices, nurtured without benefit of introduction, and I was advised by them to be particularly courteous to Justice Marshall.

We were on final descent, a few thousand feet off the ground, when I circulated down the aisle informing House Speaker Carl Albert, senators Lloyd Bentsen and Hubert Humphrey, and the rest about the Veep's wishes. I said to Justice Marshall, "Sir, the Vice President would like you and Mrs. Marshall to deplane from the front door."

He looked me straight in the eye and, in the most judicial of tones, solemnly proclaimed, "No doubt the Vice President would very much like me to do just that, and right now!"

Agnew got a chuckle out of the exchange and said he was delighted to know that even liberals had a sense of humor.

The dedication ceremony was a three-ring circus. With President Nixon, former President Johnson, and Vice President Agnew all present, there were Secret Service agents and aides all over the place. It looked like a convention of hearing-aid demonstrators. I had the feeling they were all protecting each other from themselves. There was a large crowd before any of the invited guests arrived.

As it happens, there is always a certain amount of ranking protocol and good, old-fashioned rivalry between the presidential and vice-presidential aides and their Secret Service staffs. Whether they'll ever break stride and admit it themselves, the aides on the President's staff consider themselves a full notch above the boys who work for the Vice President. And they, in turn, consider themselves a notch above the former president's staff, who fancy themselves as somehow better than the staffers who watch out for the President's wife and kids.

The walkie-talkies were running out of frequencies that day in Austin. As the teams scrambled and crisscrossed in each other's path, it became a tug-of-war. On occasion, tempers would flare. But just say, "This is for the President," and almost any argument would stop short.

Almost. I recall an incident that occurred in Washington a short time later, when I was looking at the same situation all over again. In a joint appearance at a big GOP luncheon, Nixon and Agnew were to use the same holding room. Agnew was to use it first and then appear on stage. Nixon would follow him into the room shortly after, make his appearance, and leave.

I was busy preparing the standard setup for Agnew: a bottle of water, a bottle of Chivas, some soda, ice, and coffee. Agnew enjoyed having beverage options in the holding room, and although he seldom drank in the afternoon, he liked his room set up that way. When Nixon's advance people arrived, they were adamant about changing it all. They had a much stricter, tighter set of do's and don'ts and wouldn't put a single extra flower in the room if Nixon didn't want it.

When the rhubarb started, I explained that when Agnew was finished with the room, we would remove everything and they could then readjust the facilities any way they wanted. This was considered the height of unreason by Nixon's people, who insisted the holding room be set up from the start exactly as the President wanted it. I balked, but they held firm and there has never been a bigger tempest over a more insignificant coffeepot.

As it turned out, the President and Vice President were in the room for less than two minutes each. Neither used anything and, in fact, breezed through without a glance.

Following the dedication, President Johnson gave the Agnews a personal tour of the library's facilities. It is magnificent, consistent with the image of the big Texan. At one point during the tour, Johnson thoughtfully noticed that my view was obscured by him and the Vice

President. (Being only five-eight, I was like a ficus behind two redwoods.) He gestured to me and said, "C'mon now, Petah, get right in here. I don't want you tah miss ah thing." He was so proud of his library that he couldn't stand the idea of even a humble vice-presidential aide not seeing everything.

I wasn't invited but, with the help of my White House pass, sneaked in to Tricia Nixon and Eddie Cox's wedding on June 12, 1971. I really didn't sneak in—I escorted my Aunt Dolores (who *was* asked) as far as the receiving line and then I split. By early evening, the Agnews, Dolores Hope, Henry Kissinger, the Art Linkletters, and our staff departed on Air Force Two for Los Angeles. Later that night, the Agnews attended the Association of the U.S. Army Ball at the Beverly Hilton Hotel, where Bob Hope was the guest of honor.

For months prior to this event, I had urged Bob repeatedly to interview Ray Siller, a comedy writer who was cranking out some of Agnew's best one-liners, but for far less money than writer's scale. Ray's writing kept the staff in stitches and audiences loved this candid new aspect of the austere-appearing Vice President. Even the occasionally hostile news media would look forward to Agnew's opening barbs. I can count on my thumb the number of times I dared to badger my uncle about anything, especially on matters concerning his profession, but out of sheer admiration for Siller's ability, I felt compelled to go out on a limb and push the guy's talent as far as I could.

The night of the Army Ball, Agnew took the podium first while Hope and I sat back to listen. As most comedians know, there are certain topical jokes of the day, or spoofs of the morning headlines, that always get big laughs. Indeed, Hope has built a tremendous career on this particular aspect of humor. But once a specific topic has been teased, any subsequent mention of it to the audience is old news. One by one, Agnew successfully delivered a Siller-written wisecrack that tackled most of the news *du jour*. The military audience howled.

I looked down and saw Hope scribbling on a napkin and then making quick check marks at every timely joke that Agnew made. He turned to me and, out of the corner of his mouth, he whispered, "Who the hell is writing his material?"

"That's Ray Siller! The guy I've been telling you about for months!" Hope shook his head and laughed, "Tell him he's hired!"

After the gala, the Agnew entourage departed for Palm Springs and what was now our permanent headquarters at Sinatra's. This was a night to turn in immediately, as the next day was surely to be an exhausting one.

June 13, 1971, marked the day Frank Sinatra was to go into retirement. (For two and a half years, anyway.) In the mid-afternoon, we departed for Los Angeles with Frank on Air Force Two for that occasion.

After dinner with the Ronald Reagans at their Pacific Palisades home, we drove to the Ahmanson Theater at the Los Angeles County Music Center where Frank was to give a final performance and officially announce his decision to retire. The whole evening was touching, but perhaps it was Roz Russell who best epitomized what was happening. She was visibly moved on stage, unashamedly crying because Frank, one of her closest friends, was leaving the business. She and her husband, Freddie Brisson, hosted a stunning party afterwards. I was driving to their home in the motorcade and, by coincidence, Henry Kissinger and I wound up in the same car. I had met him several times in Washington and was beginning to enjoy his company on a social level. I asked Henry how he and Sinatra met.

He said, "It's very simple. Ve vere at a party one night—a typical Hollyvood party at Kirk Douglas's. Frank and I vere the only real people in the room. It vas inevitable that ve should meet. Great men alvays get together."

We returned to the compound very late. One nightcap later, the Agnews exited to bed, and Frank and I had a Stolichnaya night. Of the late, one-to-one drinking bouts we had, this one stands out vividly. Frank was relaxed, a bit introspective, but at peace with himself. After fifty-eight films, one hundred or more albums, and some two thousand individual recordings, he deserved a rest.

Frank told me that as a kid he used to swim underwater in the New Jersey public pools to increase his lung capacity. He showed me how Tommy Dorsey stole a breath for a long trombone passage by quickly sucking in air from the side of his mouth. He said that by watching Dorsey, he learned the technique that enabled him to phrase verse the way he does. In his early days, twelve shows a day was the norm, making breath control a matter of necessity.

I was startled when Frank told me that he had done active

work for the CIA during the Johnson years. He mentioned it in passing and did not elaborate, nor did I delve deeper. Earlier that year, 1971, I was given access to a Justice Department file on Sinatra, which is often obliquely referred to by the press as "the" file on Sinatra. It dated back to the Robert Kennedy years. Reading through, it became obvious to me that Frank's association with the underworld syndicate was, at worst, an arm's length away.

In my opinion, Sinatra's apparent fascination with the underworld is akin to the kind of thing that occurs when a kid watches an old Jimmy Cagney movie on TV: There's an offbeat attraction toward the daring bad guys. Those close to Frank understand his somewhat romantic attitude toward underworld figures. And certainly the "criminal-as-hero" idea is not uncommon, as the success of Arthur Penn's film *Bonnie and Clyde* proved. As for Sinatra's much-publicized "criminal associates," I think it's only fair to point out that working in the entertainment business, especially around Las Vegas, he professionally knew, and by default, was bound to associate with some of the murkier figures who often owned the establishments he performed in. They signed the paychecks.

The file I saw was conjecture and nothing in the entire report pointed to any direct or underhanded involvement by Frank. There was no mention, by the way, of Frank's connection with the CIA, so Frank's comment was a real surprise to me. Yet it's not impossible. Sinatra is a patriot and proudly would do whatever he was asked in order to serve his country.

With the chirping of the desert birds getting louder, our conversation ended. Frank retired for the second time that night, and I took a walk in the warm morning air.

We basked in the sun for two more days and returned to Washington. The Vice President prepared for his forthcoming trip around the world, and I had a chance to send my clothes to the laundry. In late June, Agnew departed on his global tour, with domestic stops in Phoenix and Palm Springs. He rested for a few days at our usual desert retreat and left to circle the world. I took leave with instructions to rejoin the Vice President in Madrid, Spain, at the end of July. Several days later, I flew back to Washington with Frank aboard his Gulfstream G-2 jet. Air Force Two, the name designated for any plane the Vice President is aboard, is usually a plush aircraft with the latest equipment and the finest accommodations. But even Air Force Two would have to go far to top the luxury in which Frank transported himself.

The interior of his jet was designed by him, and it showed. The forward compartment was comfortably appointed with plush seats which opened into beds. The main compartment, done entirely in his favorite colors of burnt orange and chocolate brown, had a large sofa bed, an executive chair, a desk with a communications console, and rich wood tables. The electronic instrumentation was equivalent to the sophisticated gear on the jet used by the Vice President. The head, with its brass and gold fixtures, was bigger than the one in my first apartment.

With several members of Agnew's family and a couple of friends, we departed L.A. for Washington. On June 30, Sinatra was honored in the Senate by such distinguished members as Hubert Humphrey, Ed Muskie, Claiborne Pell, Jacob Javits, and John Tunney. The tribute entered into the *Congressional Record* was very moving.

The following week, Frank, Tina Sinatra, and I were sitting in Rumpelmayer's near the Park Lane Hotel in New York. It was midafternoon and we ordered a round of tuna fish sandwiches and milkshakes. A cute little girl came in with her nicely dressed mother, and they sat down at a table near ours. In front of the cashier's counter was a row of huge stuffed animals, all of them larger than the little girl. She noticed a gigantic white Snoopy and immediately asked her mother for it. The mother was very understanding and explained that, if she waited for Christmas, maybe Santa would bring it to her. But the little girl was persistent. And so was the mother: It was an expensive $60 toy.

Tina and I were aware of this byplay between mother and daughter because we faced them, but Frank seemed unaware, facing the other way and involved in our own conversation. The rest was background noise to him.

We finished our lunch about the same time as our neighbors. Frank excused himself and got up to pay the check. As usual, the cashier, like most people, seemed to have something to say to FAS, as Tina and I waltzed outside to our waiting limousine.

The next thing we saw from our limo was the mother, the daughter, and Snoopy coming out of Rumpelmayer's. The cashier had been instructed to give the girl the dog and to tell her that Santa Claus had overheard her. Both Tina and I smiled as a very happy little girl carried a stuffed Snoopy bigger than herself while a bewildered, head-turning mother tried to figure out who Santa Claus really was.

For the next two and a half weeks, I was treated to a way of life that could only be created by Frank Sinatra. Obviously, Sinatra is enormously wealthy, and few people have ever worked harder for their wealth or deserved it more. But it's not Frank's millions that are impressive; it's the way he uses them. As the two of us crossed the Atlantic on his jet, I realized more than ever that the true secret of Frank's life-style lies not so much in its luxury—which is overwhelming—but in its unpretentious flair, its continuous easy charm. It is a perfect extension of the man's personality.

The flight engineer/steward had turned down our beds in each compartment, but we never used them; there was too much to talk about. As I sat munching one of New York's finest pizzas and sipping a vintage Ruffino reserve, I couldn't help thinking of old Lindy eating a stale sandwich and freezing his ass off flying the same route. Seven hours later, the west was still in blackness as sunrise peeked over the coast of Ireland. We landed peacefully at Gatwick.

From there, we took a helicopter to London, where a chauffeur-driven, four-door Jaguar with smoked windows awaited us. The English enthusiasm for Sinatra was even more intense and demonstrative than America's. Crowds gathered so quickly that they actually proved to be a minor safety problem whenever Frank walked around London. But Frank has a kind of sixth sense about crowds: He seems able to tell, before it happens, when a crowd is going to get too big to handle. You learn, when crowds do gather, to move when Frank moves. To dawdle can cost you cabfare to catch up with him.

Shopping with Sinatra can be an unsettling experience. In the course of browsing through a store, if you pointedly or inadvertently mention something is beautiful or say, "My, isn't that nice!" don't be surprised if it's back at the hotel before you get there. Once we dashed into Dunhill's for cigarettes and I slipped, commenting on how attractive a gold-inlaid, tortoise-shell lighter was. When we returned to Claridge's for cocktails at five, a messenger arrived with a box containing the lighter I'd casually admired. I was constantly with Sinatra that day, and I still can't figure out how he bought it and arranged for its delivery.

That first evening we took in Anabel's, probably the finest private club I've seen. It is dreadfully black-tieish, slightly English foppish, but still a swinging, swank place with good food. At that time, it was way ahead of anything in the States. We had drinks with Cubby Broccoli, an affable and gentle man who, despite some early misfortune, was now back on top since his friendship with Ian Fleming had allowed him to produce the early 007 stories in England. (I was told that some ancestors of Broccoli's were responsible for the hybrid of the same name.)

I had never been at the American Embassy in London before Walter Annenberg took over, but I understood it had been quite rundown. If so, Walter had done a spectacular job of restoring the place. He gave Frank and me a tour, and it was obvious that a lot of attention was given to the art collection. I thought that the many pieces loaned or donated by Walter and his wife, Lee, added a lot to the fairly staid atmosphere of the place, but Sinatra obviously had reservations about some of the abstract impressionist works that hung there. Every now and then he'd flash me his "get-a-load-of-that" look.

It has been said that the Annenbergs had found it difficult at first to be accepted in London, but there was no evidence of that when we were there, and it was clear that Ambassador Annenberg was doing a good job. That he was a good administrator shouldn't have surprised anyone: His newspaper dynasty in Philadelphia and the meteoric success of *TV Guide* were visible tokens of his great ability.

We took off for Nice, but the French air-traffic controllers were on a work slowdown, and we were instructed not to cross French airspace. After conferring with his pilots, Frank said, "To hell with the air controllers. We're going! We've got dinner plans tonight, and I'm not going to fool around flying along the edges of France."

It was a tense ride for us. I was "casually" instructed to keep an eye out for other aircraft. No one ever flew across *la belle France* in a jet any lower than we did. I could count the chickens on the farms and I was sure that when we landed in Nice there would be a welcoming committee of *gendarmes.* But all that was there was a limo and baggage car, and soon we were whizzing down the scenic, winding drive along the Côte d'Azur to Monaco.

For the next couple of days, we enjoyed the hospitality of Henry and Nancy Ittleson, close friends of Frank's from New York and Palm Springs, at their picturesque villa. Soon we were joined by

Barbara Marx and her son Bobby, who were just ending a European holiday.

Sunning on the beach one day, Frank asked us where we'd like to go for dinner. No suggestions surfaced, so he made one of his own. "Let's go see my friend Johnny Piquet." Jean-Pierre Piquet was the general manager at the Athens Hilton, and Frank was godfather to J.P.'s son. The idea certainly met no resistance. "Peter," he said, "please call the crew and tell them to file a flight plan for Athens with a 7:30 wheels up." So off we went.

An hour and a half later, we landed in Greece. The limos were waiting, and by 10:00 we were dining on the roof of the Athens Hilton under a huge full moon, while strolling violinists serenaded us with "Strangers in the Night." High above us, the ageless Acropolis loomed, luminous in the moonlight. A typical evening with Sinatra.

We stayed over, were up by ten, and back on the beach at Monaco by mid-afternoon. Frank sent the plane back to London that day to pick up daughter Tina and her beau, actor Robert Wagner. Flying into Nice, Tina was overwhelmed by the dazzling display of fireworks that illuminated the Côte d'Azur. Knowing her father's fetish for pyrotechnics, she was convinced that Daddy had really outdone himself on her behalf. Wagner hated to destroy her fantasy but reminded her that July 14 was Bastille Day and that Daddy Frank, as swell as he was, didn't have much to do with the French Revolution.

Later that evening, we all went to the Sporting Club, Henry Ittleson's favorite casino. He played baccarat every night he was there. (In fact, they told me that when he passed away a few years ago they turned his chair face down on the table.) While Henry was playing baccarat, Frank decided that we should have some walking around money and gave me a check for $25,000. I cashed it, gave him back his money, and went on to the roulette wheel to play.

Roulette is my favorite game of chance. I like to sit at the wheel with the equivalent of $100 in five-franc chips. That's my kind of gambling. I can lounge there all evening and have a grand time. Champagne is brought to you and your cigarettes are lit for you, which to me makes for a very civilized way to gamble.

Over my shoulder, I heard that familiar voice say, "Two thousand dollars on the rouge." There was a signal from the wheel boss to lift the limit. The little ball jumped, sure enough, into the red five, and Frank said, "Give the chips to my pal. He's never going to buy a Citroën the way he's playing with those five-franc chips down there."

Everyone at the table stared, and after a slight protest I said, "Frank, thanks. See you later."

As luck would have it, I went on that night with the $2,000 of Frank's money and the $110 of my own and parlayed it into an incredible amount of loot. When I finally got up from the table, I had a pile of chips the size of tarot cards in denominations of five and ten thousand francs. I went into the bar, where I found Frank at a table. He saw my winnings and commented, "It looks like you'll be able to buy Citroëns in matching decorator colors!"

Then he said, "Give me one of those things. The table . . . this damn thing . . . is rocking, and a matchbook won't do it." With that, he reached over and took a ten-thousand-franc chip and stuck it under the leg so the table wouldn't wobble. I tell you, I never left that table, not even long enough to go to the men's room.

While we were having our drink, I thought, I've got to give Frank back his money, but not to make a scene, I'll wait until later. When I cashed in, the largest bill they had in the casino was five hundred francs, which at the time came to about $100. I had francs coming out of every pocket. We went downstairs to Régine's club, Jimmy's, a swinging discotheque on a lagoon facing the Mediterranean. I picked up the check and, for the first time, I had an idea of how expensive things were. We had gone to Jimmy's every night; it was part of the program. There was always an automatic setup on Frank's table—two bottles of Dom Perignon, a bottle of Jack Daniels Black, a bottle of Stolichnaya, and mixers. If anybody wanted something else, all he or she had to do was ask, but that was the standard setup. We only did a modest bit of drinking that night, but, with just eight of us, the bill rolled in at $700. I figured that was the average check every night for drinks at Jimmy's. I couldn't even imagine how much the rest of a full day's program came to.

From there, we went to a smaller disco. By that time, I could have walked on water, and the next thing I clearly remember is waking up in my suite in the Hotel de Paris to the sound of Sinatra's familiar voice. My blurry eyes informed me that, incredibly, there was a very pretty girl on each side of me and francs scattered all over the room. F.S. stood in the doorway, shook his head, and said, "My, my! Who said money can't buy everything?"

Now fully awake and in something of a state of shock, I began to try to reassemble my fragmentary memories of the night before. I had gone to still another disco and met these two little ladies whose amateur standing I had never questioned—after all, they hadn't asked for anything. But then, I never really knew, since I don't speak French and Dom Perignon is still no substitute for Berlitz. Frank had gone back to the hotel to retire and I had continued to party until the wee hours of the morning. Somehow I had wound up with this little *ménage à trois* in the suite and, apparently carried away with the occasion, had scattered francs all over the room, confetti-style.

I kissed the girls good-bye and ceremoniously proceeded into Frank's room. "Frank," I said, "you've got to take this money back. It's really yours."

"What the hell do I want it for?" he replied. "Buy a monopoly set—it's the same thing."

Another memory I cherish from that astonishing trip concerns a character at the beach club who had a habit of constantly walking back and forth in front of our lounge chairs. He was a nondescript Frenchman who had a deck chair several rows down from ours, and he always had a portable radio glued to his ear. He would take methodical strolls, radio in hand, and you could practically set your watch by the movements of this guy who never took his eyes off Frank. Sinatra dubbed him "Charlie Radio." We figured, if he was going to be a mild nuisance, we might as well enjoy the absurdity of it. Every day, Charlie Radio got a deck chair a seat or two closer to our regular spot. (Saving himself a few steps, I guess.)

Frank has eyes in the back of his head when he needs to. He said to me, without looking up from his crossword puzzle, "Charlie Radio is just inching along. By Friday, he's going to make contact."

On Thursday, he was a couple of chairs closer. That night, we stayed around Monaco and took in the Sporting Club. Who should walk in but attentive "Mr. Charlie" in black tie, *sans* radio. Frank spotted him right away, walked up to him, and gave him a hearty slap on the back. "Hello there, Charlie Radio. I just thought I'd get to you, pal, before you got to me tomorrow." Startled and pale-faced, he never uttered a word. The beach on Friday seemed empty without him.

It was in Monaco that I first learned of Frank's talent as an artist. I was keenly aware of his fine appreciation of art, but I did not know that he himself was so skilled. We were having a late night, or practically speaking an early morning, plate of linguine with white clam sauce at one of the cozy outdoor bistros near the hotel. The tablecloth was brown shopping paper, and as fast as Frank would pencil-sketch the surroundings, Tina and I would grab for a "masterpiece," which the laughing artist would sign "F. Sinatra." I later learned that Frank's clown oils are much valued by the few friends who possess them.

The wonderful days on the Riviera rolled on. Before leaving on this trip, we had seen Henry Kissinger in Washington and we told him when we would be in Monte Carlo. He said he was going to be in Paris about the same time. Frank was enthusiastic. "We'll take the plane to Paris and meet you for dinner at Maxim's." Henry pinned down a date and said to call him in Paris. On the given date, I placed a call to the George V where he was to be staying.

I reached several concerned voices on the phone, emphatically denying that Mr. Kissinger was even expected in Paris. Thinking the hotel might be a little slow, I called Henry's office in Washington and was shifted from one formal voice to another. One very staunch baritone demanded to know whom he was speaking with. "This is Peter Malatesta. Frank Sinatra and I are in Monte Carlo, and we've made arrangements with Dr. Kissinger to meet him in Paris this evening for dinner. Where is he?"

I could tell there was something amiss. "Oh no, you're wrong. He's nowhere near there." The baritone was reluctant to disclose his whereabouts, but did mumble something to the effect that Kissinger was making a series of speeches in Seattle.

Frank smelled a rat. "Something's up, Peter." The day after our calls, Henry was indeed in Paris and all over the front pages of the European newspapers. He was returning from his secret mission to China. We had had his staff in a flutter, wondering how the hell we knew Kissinger was to be in Paris. Obviously, he hadn't told us what he was going to be doing before our dinner date, but apparently his staff thought we had somehow got hold of top-secret information.

The day before I left Monaco to rejoin the Vice President in Spain, Fritz Loew took us motorsailing along the Riviera coast on his majestic yacht. The afterdeck was the scene for a lavish buffet lunch, abundant with fresh fruits and vegetables that just taste better in France than anywhere else in the world. Loew, the composer of such great musicals as *Camelot,* brought a cluster of young beauties with him who would have made old King Arthur wish he were still a prince.

At last my incredible holiday ended and I was flown, alone, on "Sinatra One," to meet Air Force Two in Madrid. The Vice President arrived from Kinshasa, Zaire, and Mrs. Agnew, who had toured Europe independently, arrived from Rome. Among us we had a night full of stories to tell.

Being in Washington, even in the sticky August heat, was a relief. Since working for Agnew, I hadn't spent two consecutive weeks on my home turf. The Agnews traveled to Ocean City, Maryland, almost every weekend that August. Although frequently invited to join them, I disliked the three miles of "condo canyons" that the resort offered and chose, instead, to spend my free weekends discovering new social ties in D.C.

Louise Gore, my astute Maryland political friend, was kind enough to introduce me to the circle of Washington socialites she enjoyed. I was pleased to be included in her intimate dinner parties at the Jockey Club, which Louise's family owned. With never more than ten guests, Gore's dinners enabled you to really get to know who you were sharing champagne with.

It was there that I was introduced to the legendary and charming Perle Mesta. Leaning over her dessert, she told me that it was about time that men, other than the diplomats, became involved in hosting Washington parties.

"Peter," she said, "if you're entertaining just to have fun, you're wasting your time. Parties are what makes Washington work. Remember that."

Historically, the city of Washington used to be relatively quiet. I learned that the mighty white-marbled seat of American government hadn't really started to swing at all until, of all things, Prohibition! When booze was legally proclaimed taboo, the embassies had a field day. Legally classified as foreign soil, they were suddenly given an unprecedented social advantage—they could serve drinks all day and night if they were so inclined. People fought for invitations.

Once Prohibition ended, the format and pace of having parties, and getting business accomplished through them, was well-established. In the forties, the phenomenon of the great hostesses emerged as private money began its quest to court the powers in public life.

Old Washington, which means anyone wealthy who lived in town before or during the time of FDR, were dubbed "the cave-dwellers." Because this self-contained clique entertained mostly themselves, other ways and means had to be found to expand the party circuit.

Mesta cut sharply into the cavedwellers by being a popular outsider who started a social trend that spread quickly. Suddenly, it seemed that every lawyer's wife in town had to host whatever events she could in order to further her own social standing and broaden the party horizon for all.

Parties became useful for government. Where else could an attorney general chat with a leading Supreme Court justice without raising legal eyebrows? A party is a perfect cover, because there's no law that dictates who an ambitious host or hostess may or may not invite. While two publicly antagonistic guests from Capitol Hill might be criticized for having been seen together at lunch or in a private bull session at the office, who could gripe if they just happened to be at the same cocktail soirée?

Although private from the public at large, parties spread gossip quickly among insiders. Items and tidbits that never could be published or disseminated by conventional means were the main course in any successful Capital gathering. The city's leading social and political powers seemed to have an insatiable desire to know who was doing what with whom; what was coming down the road next; who was in and who, most definitely, was out.

Mesta's leading social competitor in her heyday was Marjorie Merriweather Post, who often adorned her famed gatherings with a string quartet in the drawing room, thus suffocating conversation and gossip. Perle never made such a mistake: She geared everything toward chatter. After dinner, all she wanted her guests to do, besides a little dancing, was to chew the fat with so-and-so. They loved it and called her "Madam."

I was one of the last converts to the Mesta style before she retired to Oklahoma. She lit a social torch in me that would illuminate my path to Embassy Row. I knew, since my successful reception for Sinatra at Taloe House, that when the proper time came, I could slide out from being an aide and make a social position for myself in Washington. Between Perle's advice and my instincts, I was beginning to get a better feel for D.C. society but I still needed to find out what the total picture was, and how this town's black-tie crowd operated. In short, I wanted to partake in the role Perle had created; after all, my guest towels had "PM" on them too. For the time being, however, I put her advice in my back pocket, as I faced a rigorous traveling schedule with the Vice President.

September was a "sporting" month for the staff. Agnew joined Jackie Gleason in Miami, Florida, to have some fun and a round of golf at Inverary Golf Club. Jackie was building a new home there at the time and proudly described it as having one bedroom and five bars in six thousand square feet. As he pointed out, "You're never more than twenty feet from a drink."

The three of us had a golf cart stacked with plenty of booze and golf balls—when you play with Gleason, you need both. "The Great One" appeared to be a bit overbearing and blunt with the people who worked for him; he was a feisty host, but a good one.

We later played golf with Arnold Palmer in Latrobe, Pennsylvania. Arnie wasted no time in reminding Spiro and me how the two of us had gotten into a little trouble several years before. Palmer was then a young, dashing champion on the way up, had just been named "Golfer of the Year," and had subsequently been asked to appear on a Hope TV show which also guest-starred Dean Martin. Weaned on golf, I took an immediate shine to the sport's hottest rising star and enjoyed talking with him backstage.

After a smooth rehearsal with the TV crew, the show took an hour and a half break. Arnie and I skipped dinner and wandered over to Dean Martin's dressing room. Dean was amiable, and Arnie was excited about meeting the star. Dean broke out the booze and although we only had two or three apiece, it was still Dean Martin doing the pouring.

The time came for Arnie to tape his dialogue with Hope. Where he'd been so perfect in the run-through, Arnie was now unable to banter with Hope on camera without roaring at every little thing Bob said or did. Helpless with laughter, it was obvious Arnie was not going to make it through the taping. Hope called for another short break and then grabbed my arm and quickly pulled me aside.

"What the hell did you do with Palmer?"

"I didn't do anything to Palmer!"

"Where did you guys go?"

"Oh, we just sat around with Dean Martin for a little while," I said, feeling my tail getting stuck between my legs.

Hope rolled his eyes heavenward. "You're kidding!"

After a cup of coffee and a cold spash of water, Arnie was fine and the show continued without a problem. Afterward, Hope called me aside again, warning, "Don't you ever bring anyone into Dean Martin's dressing room on one of *my* shows again—especially one of these young kids; you'll corrupt 'em!"

As September progressed, there was a golfing stopover in Palm Springs en route to the eighteenth National Convention of the Society of Former Special Agents of the FBI in Atlanta, Georgia. This was the first time I met then-governor Jimmy Carter. The thing that stands out from that meeting is that nothing stands out. During my travels with Agnew, I kept a fairly meticulous journal, remarking on each politician I dealt with. When reviewing my notes on that meeting with Carter, I found a conspicuously blank page, except for the mention of his name.

I celebrated my birthday on October 7 in Buffalo, New York, with Agnew. We attended a fund raiser honoring Republican Congressman Jack Kemp.

Kemp cut a good figure. The elders of the party were impressed with the way the young conservative and former Buffalo Bills quarterback dealt with the hierarchy, as if he had grown up with them. He conversed easily about sticky political issues and I had the feeling I was talking to All-American Kemp and not another congressman. Agnew was impressed with the way the folks in Buffalo enthusiastically welcomed their own representative and he whispered to me, "This one's going to be President one day; just watch!"

After that, we spent a quiet, preparatory week before the Veep embarked on an exceptional European tour for the duration of the month.

We started the trip, which was to climax in Greece, by visiting Ankara, Turkey. If I never get up in the morning again to the sooty smell created by the burning of soft coal, it will be too soon! So much for Ankara!

By contrast, no specific international function I attended was more colorful or memorable than the celebration held in Persepolis commemorating the 2,500th anniversary of the Persian Empire. The voluminous accounts given by the press barely did credit to the occasion. The ancient ruins of Cyrus the Great's palace city were turned into an extravagant fantasyland. Every detail of the program was prepared with care and imagination. The actual campsite was nestled in the foothills of the Zagros Mountains, a short distance from Persepolis itself and removed from the desert heat of the Marvdasht basin where the ruins lie. The heart of the camp covered an area of five city blocks, encircled by a periphery of armed troops. Within the core, colorfully striped tents formed a self-sufficient oasis—each tent flying the flag of its guest nation. These canvas palaces had an unobstructed view of the desert with no hint of the surrounding security barriers. Crisscrossed with foliage and walkways, the site was breathtaking.

The lavishness, both in the tents and out out, was staggering. Acres of Persian carpets stretched below ornate Middle-Eastern chandeliers. A grand main tent rose like a cathedral in the center. Everything eaten and drunk there was catered by Maxim's of Paris.

The entire episode left me fascinated and spellbound. When again, I wondered as I toyed with a silver urn of beluga caviar and toast, would so many world leaders and figureheads be gathered in such an unworldly retreat at the same time? The uniqueness of the situation was heightened by the fact that each leader was entitled to only one full-time aide within the camp, besides a personal valet. Other staffers in the entourage were located in hotels or at the University of Shiraz some forty miles away. Those aides situated outside "Shangri-la" commuted by bus each day. Vice President Agnew represented the United States, and I, fortunately, was given access to all the camp's extraordinary activities.

As ludicrous as it seems, each leader brought along his nation's automobile. Prince Philip tooled around in a Rolls Royce, driving it a total of two blocks to the main tent. Mr. Agnew was given a Chevrolet. At whose direction it was to supply us with a Chevy is unknown; I guess they thought that was what America was all about. At least it was a four-door sedan and not a Nova coupe.

The afternoon Iranian sun can be insufferably hot. One afternoon, to cure a gigantic thirst attack, I wandered into the grand tent. There were no other guests present, only a battalion of Maxim's finest waiting for someone, anyone, to walk in. Without being asked, they spontaneously rushed over an iced bottle of Dom Perignon—superb refreshment on a blistering day, especially when touched with a bit of fresh orange juice.

In came a familiar stranger, Emperor Haile Selassie. I started running through my memory for the proper salutation. I could not remember the State Department briefing, but assumed I should avoid such greetings as "Hi, Your Emperor!" I did, however, seem to recall that one couldn't go very wrong calling anyone "sir," so I took a chance that the world's only emperor would not be offended by being called that.

He wasn't, and we wound up having a remarkably pleasant chat. His praise, through his interpreter, for the United States was profuse, and he showed a true liking for the Vice President. He seemed relaxed and, to my amazement, was perfectly content to kill some time in the main tent engaging in trivialities with me. Through some verbal tangent, the game of backgammon entered our conversation. I always carried a small board with me in my luggage, as the game had become a fad with several of Agnew's aides. I found myself saying, "Just a minute, sir. Don't go away, I'll be right back." As I rushed back to the Vice President's tent, it hit me that I had just told an emperor to wait around for me! But in that atmosphere, it was difficult not to be casual.

We played a game and he told me about Ethiopia, a nation that I had previously known in name only. When, a few years later, I heard of my erstwhile backgammon partner's demise, I almost felt as though I'd lost a friend.

Other encounters were not quite so exclusive. Then-Prince Juan and Princess Sophia of Spain and I renewed an acquaintance we had made at an Apollo launching in Florida. Prince Philip was as charming and poised as the press indicates. As for the shah, he tended to shy away from the world's fanciest tent city and made appearances only when officially scheduled. Otherwise, he stayed in his downtown palace in Teheran.

One night, we had a sound-and-light show displayed amid the ruins of Persepolis. In that setting, under the stars, it was easy to fantasize the presence of Alexander the Great. With his horns blasting in the distance, I imagined his troops gloriously approaching the city. The display left even royalty breathless.

The finale parade was as lavish as the camp it marched

through that afternoon. All the world principals, in full regalia, sat in a row on one side of the main boulevard. Across the street were the international press and aides, I loitered around all morning, aiming to get myself a prime spot for the "parade of parades," which is how it was billed.

Five minutes before the event started, I ran into journalist Sally Quinn, covering for *The Washington Post.* Sally, suffering from the heat, was in a miserable mood. The press facilities were badly organized, and everyone seemed to be scrambling for a strategic location. I had had a great seat staked out—three feet above the others on a television platform with cameras above me—but Sally had always been pleasant to me back home, and I felt that now chivalry could not be withheld. I offered her my coveted seat, which she promptly accepted.

So I missed most of the parade and had to content myself with the next best thing. After watching enough of what I could see, I slipped back to the tent, kicked off my shoes, listened to the music from afar, and worked on another bottle of Dom.

With Persepolis now history, we journeyed on to Greece. Agnew and his entourage booked into the Athens Hilton. My memory was still fresh from the lively dinner I had had with Sinatra and the gang a few months before. Jean-Pierre again provided a pleasant repast on the roof, but some moments are not to be repeated. The view, the moon, and the food were the same, but the mood belonged to another rare moment of the past.

This stay at the Hilton was not without its merits. Arnaud DeBorchgrave introduced himself. As a senior foreign correspondent for *Newsweek*, he was awesome in his vast understanding of the political structure of western Europe. I found him surprisingly conservative, but as he put it, "The fact that I interview and write for *Newsweek* is irrelevant. I report events as they happen. My personal beliefs are my own and they [*Newsweek*] do nothing to dissuade me from them."

Arnaud questioned the timing of Agnew's trip to Greece, as he felt the reign of Papadopoulos was in serious jeopardy. The real reason for this trip, I explained, was not to pry into Greece's domestic affairs; it was simply the homecoming of a man who wanted to visit the birthplace of his father. Agnew, in a word, was doing a *Roots* number. He was received like a god in Athens. Nevertheless, the visit caused some problems between Henry Kissinger and Agnew.

Kissinger had been dead set against the trip for the same

reasons mentioned by DeBorchgrave, even though Spiro clearly stated his visit was purely a personal one. The muscle play between the two wavered back and forth, but Agnew was determined that he was going to Greece and that was that. (Perhaps it was Henry who arranged for the Chevy in Iran.)

As it turned out, the Vice President did do at least one thing that was not personal. It was the only time in my service that Agnew used a decoy maneuver to get rid of the press and his staff. We were being followed, as on any foreign trip, by a coterie of press. Agnew switched cars midway, doing a 007 routine. One motorcade, followed by the press, headed for the hotel; the other, with Agnew, went on to an unscheduled meeting.

Vic Gold and I didn't realize until we were back at the Hilton that the Vice President had ditched us, taking only his senior military aide, General Mike Dunn, and his foreign adviser from the State Department. Vic was bombarded by questions from the press, and it was the only time Gold went right up the wall. The press relied on him totally, and Vic's honesty with them was paramount. He was a gregarious, tough, and dedicated press secretary, who always leveled with the media, but he wasn't afraid to say "It's none of your damn business" if it wasn't. This time he had to give the media an explanation of Agnew's disappearance, and of course he had absolutely no idea where the Vice President was.

We only learned the explanation when Agnew returned to the hotel: He had had a secret meeting with Papadopoulos. But even then the Vice President would not address himself to what he discussed in his private meeting.

That mystery notwithstanding, the most embarrassing moment in my entire career with the Vice President took place shortly after and it only proves that partying does not always further one's causes.

Arnaud DeBorchgrave introduced me to Taki Theodoracopulos, heir to a Greek shipping dynasty and a political writer. Taki was definitely a man who liked a good time and we became instant buddies. The day before Agnew and his staff were to visit the birthplace of his father, Taki invited me for lunch and cocktails on his father's yacht, one of a slew in the family fleet. Taking along a couple of the Agnew kids, we sailed to a small island and spent a very pleasant afternoon.

That evening, Taki insisted on taking me out for a night on the town in *his* Athens. He knew everybody in every place we went to, and I lost count of all the stops. While bottle after bottle of ouzo and Dom Perignon went down, I learned the delicate art of breaking dishes over my head. My skull must have gone through a full service for twelve before Taki finally rolled me into his racy sports car. Then he and his gang headed back to his plush pad.

I woke up, sprawled on a couch, with the grandfather of hangovers: whether caused by the ouzo or the plates or a combination thereof, I shall never know. My forehead was covered with welts from the dishes, and it hurt just to keep my eyes open. Taki's apartment, as lavish as a James Bond set, was blanketed with sleeping bodies—under coffee tables, the piano, everywhere. I had no idea what part of Athens I was in, but I staggered downstairs in my open shirt and wrinkled pants, with disheveled hair and battered head, and found a cab. "The Athens Hilton!" is all I muttered before I hid from the world in the back seat.

By the time I arrived, the Vice President and staff had already left on Agnew's triumphant *hejira* to his ancestor's birthplace. It was the only plane I missed during my entire professional assignment, but I knew it was the *wrong* trip to blow. I did the only thing I could do: I went to bed.

When the staff returned to the Hilton that evening, Agnew immediately drilled me with, "Where were you and what did you do last night?" I chose not to cop out and told him everything I had done. I felt it was my duty not to fudge a tale to my disappointed boss. And besides, my visibly wounded head made any cover-up inconceivable.

For months after, Agnew was to chide me about the incident every time we planned to appear at an event. "Are you going to make this one, Peter? Or are you going out and break plates over your head?"

Following our return from Greece, we checkerboarded the States for most of November, winding up in Palm Springs for Thanksgiving weekend and the dedication of Eisenhower Memorial Hospital. President Nixon was also on hand for the official opening. Again, there was the usual confusion between the presidential and vice-presidential staffs. This time, the disjunctive power plays did not stop with the formalities of the dedication. Vic Gold called it the "Battle of the Super-Egos." It started over a rather simple thing.

The Vice President was, as usual, a guest of Sinatra's, along with Ronald and Nancy Reagan. Bob Hope called me one afternoon and said, "The President's in town, and we're playing golf tomorrow. I'm thinking of a foursome. We'd like Ted to come with us. It'll be Dick, Ted, Paul Jenkins, and myself. We're playing at El Dorado."

"Fine," I replied. "I'll relay your message to the Vice President. He's outside playing tennis. Do you need an answer right now?"

"No. Tell Ted I'll get back to him later."

Agnew finished his game and came off the court. I said, "Bob called and wants you to play golf tomorrow with the President and his friend, Paul Jenkins. I think you met him—a nice fellow, good golfer."

"Sounds good, Peter, but what about Frank? I can't play golf and leave Frank alone. I'm his guest. We've played together every day. Call Bob and ask him if we can make it a fivesome."

I called Hope back a bit later. "There's a problem here. The Veep feels he's Frank's guest, and they've got a tentative golf date set for tomorrow. He doesn't want to leave Frank alone, even though the Reagans are there to keep him company. How about a fivesome?"

"That's all right." Bob said. "Tell Frank to come along. We'll play a foursome, and I'll tell Jenkins we'll catch up with him another time."

We set the tee-off time for eleven o'clock, and I hung up. A short time later, I received a call from Paul Keyes, playing his role as a Nixon confidant. Typical. He said, "The President would like to play golf, but he wants to ride with Frank." (I saw the red, or at least the yellow, flag going up.) "The President has only met Frank formally and now that Frank is such a good friend of Ted's and beginning to support Republicans, the President would like to get to know him better." Paul cautioned me to make sure the arrangements were made discreetly, "as the President doesn't want to hurt Bob's feelings."

With childlike naiveté, I commented, "That sounds reasonable. I'll take it up with the Veep."

Agnew said it was fine with him, but I knew I had better check with Hope. I called Hope back and, without telling him of Paul's presidential request, suggested that Frank and the President ride together in one golf cart.

Hope flared slightly. "Whose idea was that?"

I fumbled some inadequate answer rather than telling him straight out that the new arrangement had come directly from the

President. Hope was now annoyed with me and, in an effort to avoid any further unpleasantness, I told him I'd call back later.

I got back to Keyes and said, "Paul, that's not the way Bob wants it."

Paul curtly snapped, "You don't seem to understand, Peter. This is what the *President* wants."

"Paul," I sighed, "it's you who doesn't understand. Nixon may be President for a few years, but Bob and Dolores are family. And I'm not about to tell Uncle Bob who the hell he is or isn't going to ride in his golf cart with. . . . 'The President wants' . . . 'The President doesn't want' . . . That's bullshit!"

After an ominous pause, Paul said he'd pass my feelings on. I joined Frank and company for cocktails and recounted my brewing dilemma. No one was frazzled but me. Just before we left the compound to go out for dinner, I received a call from Bob Haldeman. Bob was absolutely dogmatic, and told me to make damn sure that the President and Frank were in the same golf cart. Click. End of conversation.

We dined at the Dunes just a few blocks from Hope's home. Instead of enjoying my meal, I wrestled with my problem. After my second martini, a brilliant solution took form. Why not add the governor of California to the match and make it a fivesome? In the world of protocol, a governor outranks both the President and the Vice President in his home state. Hope, as host, would then ride with the senior man—Governor Reagan. Nixon and Sinatra could ride together. I could ride with Agnew, or perhaps Paul Jenkins could be added if they resolved to play a sixsome. I left the Dunes Restaurant between courses and dashed over to Hope's home to unveil my latest plan.

By now, Hope had reached the threshold on his tolerance regarding any further discussion of *his* golf game. He was convinced that I had botched up the whole thing on my own. By the time I blurted out that it was Nixon's idea, he was unbelieving. I left in a hurry, depressed with my sagging aidesmanship.

The next morning, without any further input from me, two foursomes were arranged. Hope, Nixon, Paul Jenkins, and a friend of Bob's teed off on the first hole. Agnew, Reagan, Sinatra, and I teed off on the tenth hole. At the turn, we all had lunch together with splendid conversation forthcoming from all parties except me. I just sat sheepishly with my nose in the soup; it was a bad day for aides and nephews.

Through the years, starting in the early sixties, I had been around the Ronald Reagans on various occasions, both political and social. But this golfing weekend was the first time I had spent several uninterrupted days with them. Sinatra's isolated compound gave me the opportunity for a closehand view of this couple.

Reagan was his usual relaxed self, eager to hear what was on Agnew's mind—particularly in those matters that affected California's interests. He bantered freely with Sinatra and obviously held Frank in highest respect. He was warm and friendly with me, reminiscing on past incidents. This was to be a casual weekend for him, far away from Sacramento and the rancor of the state legislators.

As we both sunned and dozed poolside, my mind drifted over the previous twelve years of our acquaintanceship. My first insight into the political Ronald Reagan came in 1960, while I worked as a part-time volunteer for a conservative activist group of Los Angeles business people. Since Reagan, fellow actor George Murphy, and myself had earlier been active in Richard Nixon's unsuccessful presidential quest, we asked Murphy if he could get Ronnie to speak at one of our monthly lunches. Reagan accepted and he was a smash! Friendly, articulate, and well-informed were the marks he received from our members. You bet we asked him back!

In mid-1961, annoyed by the liberal performance of California's Republican senator Tom Kuchel, our group of "red-hot right-wingers" set out to find ourselves a candidate who could knock off Kuchel in the primary and go on to replace him in the Senate. At a late-night strategy meeting, we unanimously agreed; Ronald Reagan was the man!

Two members of the group's board of directors, Marge Turner and Dr. Bob Morrell, joined me paying a personal call on "Citizen Reagan" at his recently acquired home in Pacific Palisades. Our face-to-face session was quite pleasant, and I was re-impressed by Reagan's easygoing yet affirmative presence. His opinions were clear and well-stated when he was asked them, and I had no doubt this straightforward, uncomplicated guy really believed in what he was saying.

Nancy Reagan was there but passively quiet. They both appeared startled when we directly proposed that Ron consider letting us back him as a 1962 candidate for the Republican senatorial nomination. He agreed that Kuchel was far too liberal, but Reagan was unsure that he was ready to enter politics and take on such a challenge. "I need time to think about that one, Peter!" he laughed. "Why don't you call me back later in the week?"

It was Reagan himself who initiated the call back, and although he was obviously flattered, he shyly declined our offer, saying in essence that although the idea greatly appealed to his ego, he wasn't ready for such a momentous political hurdle.

Disappointed but undaunted, we turned our energies toward the very distinguished and conservative state's rights attorney Loyd Wright. He agreed to the Senate race only on the condition that we get Murray Chotiner to manage the campaign. Years earlier, Chotiner was the political genius behind Nixon's successful bid for the House and Senate, and although he had stayed in the background in Nixon's 1960 presidential bid, he was considered the best manager in California politics.

Chotiner took on the campaign out of professional respect for Wright but told us we had only two chances: little and none. Then right-wing political hell-raiser and tax reformer Howard Jarvis jumped in the race at the last minute and reduced our chances to none—Wright got clobbered.

In 1964, I was again back in the political arena after a crony asked me to help in Senator Barry Goldwater's visit to Southern California. Barry was on the stump for the Republican presidential nomination and I, his biggest fan, joined the bandwagon as his volunteer driver. Whether I'm behind the steering wheel or not, when I have something to say I say it, and it wasn't long before I became a full-fledged paid aide and good family friend.

I was taken on by the Goldwater machine to help orchestrate Barry's all-out push in the California presidential primary. It had become a dogfight of sorts between the conservative Arizona senator and the liberal governor of New York, Nelson Rockefeller. There had never been any love lost between these two polarized Republicans, and the California primary had become their "OK Corral," with the winner assured the Republican presidential nomination. Goldwater, at times, seemed more obsessed with crushing Rockefeller than he did at unseating Lyndon Johnson.

Midway into Goldwater's California campaign, we scanned our list of supporters and guest speakers in preparation for a primary-eve "I Love America" rally to be held at a packed Dodger Stadium. We needed a stem-winding keynote speaker, and I tossed Reagan's name into the pot of potentials. Goldwater and his senior staff liked the idea and Reagan was contacted.

In one of the best speeches of his career, a speech that many feel launched him as a viable politician, Reagan projected himself like gangbusters. I turned to Barry midway and remarked, "He'd make a hell of a vice-presidential candidate, wouldn't he?" Goldwater smiled and said, "Someday, maybe more than that!"

The night of the California primary caught the pollsters with their pants down. Goldwater was declared the winner by one network thirteen minutes after the polls closed. Barry, his wife, Peggy, and I were alone in the hotel suite when victory was predicted. All of the staff were still hustling about, preparing for a long night and a very close election. Barry's exclamation was succinct and poignant; he turned to Peggy and said, "I beat that son-of-a-bitch—the rest doesn't matter!" He hugged Peggy and patted me on the shoulder and said, "Get Reagan on the phone; this victory belongs to him too!"

A few weeks later, the night before Goldwater was to be nominated for President at the San Francisco Cow Palace, I found myself amidst frenzied excitement in our campaign suite at the Mark Hopkins Hotel. Earlier in the evening, then-Pennsylvania governor Bill Scranton's operatives had put out an eleventh hour letter denouncing Goldwater as a no-win candidate. The blood of the California primary was still flowing and although Scranton denied any knowledge of the letter, Goldwater's top aides were beside themselves. Barry had to know the latest and now!

Being the junior man on the totem pole I was appointed to enter the stern senator's private quarters and bear the bad news. Goldwater had set up a complete and sophisticated ham radio outfit in his suite and when he had a moment to himself, he'd crouch over it with headphones and talk to the world.

When I entered his hideaway, his back was toward me and I saw him bent over, listening to some scratchy sounds from far, far away. Baited by the rest of the worried staff, I had worked up a small sweat over the potential wrath to which I might be witness. He waved me in with one hand and immediately signalled me to be quiet with a "Shh. I've got this guy on from Bangkok; we're talking about airplanes."

For the next twenty-five minutes, he carried on a conversation with this Thai, three-quarters of the way around the world, while I waited to tell him that his carefully planned campaign could be on the verge of collapse. Finally taking a break, he turned around and said, "What is it, Peter?" I explained the Scranton people had put out something inappropriate and he ought to know about it. Goldwater grabbed the letter, saw my near-shivering nervousness, and scowled, "Oh, come on—enough of this crap!" He turned back to the radio. "It's more important for me to talk to *this* guy right here," he said, gesturing toward the headphones. "Tell everybody to relax; that goddamn Scranton couldn't get himself arrested."

The awaiting staff was pale with apprehension when I came out.

Over the next decade and a half, this high-velocity opponent baiting was an aspect of politics that would always bother me. In 1964 I saw Nelson Rockefeller as the heavy in the black hat, the bad guy, the liberal out to destroy America. But when I got to know him, I found that I too had fallen victim to the opponent-baiting syndrome.

Watching him in action on many occasions at governors' conferences and during Agnew visits to New York, I first began to admire my inbred arch-enemy and then grew to respect him almost without bounds. Here was a political cat who was *not* a Horatio Alger! Rockefeller was who he was: a wealthy, intelligent heir to an entire industry who devoted himself to the common good. Besides that, he was the nicest guy on the campaign trail.

Most of his contemporaries, with the exception of Goldwater and Reagan, were comparatively aloof and beyond the reach of staffers. Most people high in public life demand that everything be channelled through a few top aides or filtered through a flock of go-fers. Rocky, on the other hand, was as accommodating as possible. He never stood on ritual or protocol. If he was standing around before or after a speech, he welcomed a good joke or a funny story from anyone. You could pat him on the back, have a few laughs, and he'd unpretentiously respond with a couple of wise-ass remarks of his own. In short, he was a junior aide's delight.

I later had serious and plaguing regrets that, back in 1964, we may have frustrated his presidential ambitions irrevocably. Rocky was an empire builder who would have made a damn good president. "Hi ya, fella!" he'd say. I grew to feel that this was more than a politician's casual greeting. He really did seem prepared to be interested in and to like virtually everyone.

Even though he has a vastly different background and sharply opposing viewpoints, Ronald Reagan is a cut from the same mold. After his widely acclaimed Goldwater rally speech, I continued to see Reagan on an infrequent basis. He was always supportive of visiting conservative GOP leaders, and he never turned me down when I asked him to introduce good friends like senators Strom Thurmond, John Tower, or, of course, Barry Goldwater. During my four-times-a-year contact with him in the mid-sixties, I became more and more impressed with his smoothness. He appeared to be the most consistent personality in the business: even-tempered, perennially charming, solicitous, interested, candid, and accessible. I was not at all surprised when he was elected governor of California.

In 1968, Reagan visited the Bob Hope Desert Classic in Palm Springs and I welcomed the chance to get to know him better. He handled the most complicated questions with direct, credible answers. He appeared to be quite satisfied with his role as governor and certainly gave no signals of presidential ambition. If I had any reservations at all about Reagan's answers, it was that they sometimes seemed a little too pat, at times almost memorized. Even old pros hem and haw *sometimes*, but not Reagan; he was like a computer. As much as I liked the man, I was ever aware that he was a thoroughly professional and successful actor. I often wondered if he didn't have a highly trained absorbent mind, with great recall when cued. Even when I sat with him in the relaxed ambience of Sinatra's poolside, I still had the same feeling.

After a day in the sun and a delightful dinner, Nancy, Sr., arranged for a series of amusing after-dinner parlor games she had picked up over the years. Her assemblage of little puzzles and mind-taxers were well-received by the dozen or so guests gathered in the compound's theater.

I noticed, however, that Nancy Reagan seemed a bit cool to this kind of idle family entertainment. When the parlor games started, Ron threw himself into them with enthusiasm, a cheerful gleam in his eye, and an occasional "Oh gosh!" But Nancy Reagan's little nose went up at the end and she properly but curtly excused herself and retired.

Frank had provided a handsome, solid gold watch as the prize for the evening's best puzzle-doer. Our group, without speaking it in so many words, decided the amiable governor should win, and he did, fair and square! The look on his face made the evening a truly memorable one, and I don't think he'd have been any happier if he'd won an Oscar.

It would be very difficult for anyone with any type of open-mindedness to spend recreational time with Ronald Reagan and dislike him. His gentle, laid-back style and permanently cheerful disposition make him as good a guy to be with as you're going to find. These same qualities seem to me to have shown through during the early months of his presidency. The courage, grace, and humor with which he met the nearly successful attempt made on his life in March 1981 show more clearly than anything I can say what sort of a man Ronald Reagan really is.

My relationship with Spiro T. had developed both professionally and personally. He was a very disciplined man, serious about his responsibility as Vice President and always mindful of his physical well-being. When the after-dinner speeches were over and there was to be a breakfast the next morning, he would retire early. But every day we were on the road, regardless of what senior staff members were present, the first person in his suite in the morning would be me. This often perturbed some of the older staffers, who would sometimes ask, "Why is Peter always the first one to see the boss? What is it?"

They needn't have worried. It wasn't about world affairs or a briefing on the day's agenda at the White House. It wasn't even a discussion of the day's activities. He used to say to me, "What did you do last night and where did you go?" He was worse than my father. I suppose that he knew that when the speeches were over and he went to bed, my evening of fun began. If I thought I might be passing through these cities only once, I was determined that my once would be memorable. I love night life, and I enjoyed telling him where I went and what I did.

One morning in New York, he said as usual, "What did you do last night, Peter?"

"On 43rd Street," I said, "—no, it was West Broadway, in the Village—there is an erotic puppet show that is not to be believed."

"An erotic puppet show?"

"Yes, sir. An erotic puppet show."

"What the hell is an erotic puppet show?"

As circumspectly as possible I tried to explain about Pinocchio and his long nose.

Spiro got hysterical. "Pinocchio!?"

I provided a little more detail. The V.P. was in an uproar. "If we get finished early tonight, I want to see that show!"

We went through the day. He made his speeches and, following the usual rites, we finally finished up and returned to our suite at the Park Lane Hotel. After we briefly added up the pluses and minuses of the day, he changed the subject and asked, "Where's that erotic puppet show?"

I was dismayed. It was a conversation from early morning, and I had doubted he'd remember it. "Down on Broadway, in the lower section."

He said, "What do you think? Should we go?"

Can you imagine going out at midnight when you've got Sam Sulliman and John Simpson along? Two very straight, heavy cats; two utterly professional, longtime Secret Service agents with flawless careers who would really rather see the Vice President put on an island in a bulletproof cage for four years than make any move in New York City late at night.

I said, "John, the old man may want to make a move."

John was stern. "He does? And where does he think he wants to go?"

"Well . . . uh . . . there's a little theater on Broadway which we are thinking about that features an erotic puppet show."

John looked at me and said, "You're putting me on. Stop it!"

Dead silence.

"An erotic puppet show?" John asked, squinting. "That *he* wants to see?"

"That's right. The old man wants to see it. There's no assassination threat. A little tacky group maybe . . ."

"You're going to jeopardize his career for that?" John was angry.

"What jeopardy? It's just a fun little show. There's no danger. It's amusing."

"If that's what the old man wants to do, Peter, we'll do it. I've never told you where to take the Vice President on his free time, and I'm not going to start now. That's not the role of the Secret Service. But even JFK never pulled a stunt like this."

The moment of fun was over, and John was right. Spiro agreed and that was that. As a compromise, we went to a neat Greek place, Dionysius, and watched the dancers. It was one of the very few nights the Vice President stayed out quite late. In fact, we got back to the hotel at about 2:30 A.M.

Still in a pixyish mood, the Vice President and I laughed over a nightcap about the events leading to, and away from, the puppet show. "If you think tonight's episode is a corker, sir, you should hear what I pulled on Hope in Spain. I almost got left there!"

Agnew signaled for one last Chivas, kicked off his shoes and lent an ear. "It was my second Christmas tour with Hope," I began, "and we were staying at the Castellano Hilton in Madrid. . . ."

I asked the elevator operator, "Where do you go for flamenco dancing? I'm nutty over it!" In broken English, he explained that there was such a place. It was all Spanish and I wouldn't see any other Americans there, but it was the best place in Madrid for the action.

After the show at the Air Force base, we returned to the hotel and Hope asked me what plans I had for the evening. I told him about this flamenco place and he said, "Great! We'll all go."

Bob, Gina Lollobrigida, and several others in the cast piled into Air Force staff cars and off we went. Sure enough, no Americans, just a well-dressed local crowd. The flamenco show was everything the elevator guy bragged about and there was great enthusiasm over the arrival of Bob Hope. It was one of the rare nights that I saw Bob drink some champagne and mellow out.

There were these twin brothers who danced like they were wired together, both mentally and physically. They could have been Siamese—when one moved, the other moved. They did a flamenco routine that was not to be believed. Hope turned to me during their act and said, "These guys are just sensational, but I've gotta go and get some sleep. Get a hold of Jack and tell him to film these guys in the morning. You make the deal with them; they're just great!"

As soon as Bob and company had left, I called Jack Hope,

Bob's brother, who produced the show. It was now 3:30 in the morning. I was totally hyper and three-quarters wasted on champagne. "Jack," I said, "we've found the most marvelous act!"

He snapped back, "Where the hell are you?"

"I'm at El Duede."

"Where? Oh hell, what time is it?" He did not sound amused.

"Bob wants to film these guys," I explained. "These two flamenco dancers; they're really knock-outs."

Jack was peeved. "Are you crazy? You kept Hope out until three o'clock when we've got a day like tomorrow—today! You *gotta* be out of your mind!"

Since Jack was never nasty to me or anyone else, I could see I had him close to an all-time first. But I persisted.

Finally, he said, "Now what does Bob want to do, Peter?"

"Well, you see, Jack," I stammered, "he's gone back to the hotel but he wants *you* to film these cats tomorrow before we leave."

"That means we gotta film them at 9 A.M." Jack groaned. "You know what this is going to do? It means I gotta get our cameraman Alan Stensfold and I've got to bring the major part of the crew down there right now and set up." There was a slight pause. "If that's what Bob wants, we'll be there, but don't *you* leave!"

About forty minutes later, in came Jack, Stensfold, and several sleepy-eyed members of the production staff. We cut a deal for the brothers to dance for $500. It was now 4:30 in the morning, and my two most recent and important friends, the identical twins who spoke no English, were still dancing and Jack reluctantly acknowledged that they were indeed quite remarkable. They were so revved up by this time, they were dancing on tables, the bar, all over the place.

Jack said, "Don't let them out of your sight between now and nine o'clock or you're gonna walk home and it's a long hike from Madrid to Hollywood." With these two guys now my wards, I took them back to the hotel and up to the presidential suite, past the master bedroom where Hope was asleep, through the sitting room and into my quarters. They were still clicking their fingers and doing flamenco, this time on my bed. I called room service and ordered more champagne. It was now five o'clock and they were still having a grand time. They were teaching me flamenco without the aid of language, since I spoke almost no Spanish at all except *la cuenta, por favor* which I learned from Hope.

Anyhow, they started giggling and patting each other on the rear. No, it couldn't be, I thought. Not brothers! Brothers can't be faggots! But they were, and they had decided that now was playtime. When they motioned toward me to join them, my heart sank. It's not in any aide's manual, but you don't have to know the language to understand the action. I didn't know what to say and in my futile Spanish I tried to tell them "*No*! This is no time for a fling because it's Señor Bob Hope's suite."

They could not have misunderstood me more thoroughly. Upon hearing the name "Señor Bob Hope," they capped their drunken fantasy by charging into Hope's room, with me behind screaming, "No, no, no!" At that point, I was semi-hysterical and not only from anguish. I was laughing at the madness of the moment, and the more I laughed the more they thought for sure that this was going to be a marvelous time.

Unc was asleep in his bed under a cloud of comforters when the dynamic duo leaped onto the mattress and started dancing on his feathers. Hope popped his head out from under the covers, bellowing. "What the hell is this?"

I yelled, "They're out of control! Listen, I think they're faggots and I mentioned your name trying to hush them up and they got it all *wrong*!"

Hope, as tired as he was, had it sized up immediately and started to laugh. The more he laughed, the more the dancers were *sure* that it was going to be a magnificent morning with Señor Bob Hope and "Petee." (My new name!)

Finally, with great authority and internationally understandable finality, Bob spoke. "Get these guys, or whatever the hell they are, out of here!" With a wide, dismissive gesture, he said, "Take 'em back to your room; sober 'em up; put 'em in the shower; do anything but get them the hell out of my room!"

At last, the brothers got the point. Humble and rejected, they went back to my room where I ordered pots of coffee and quarts of orange juice.

At exactly nine o'clock, we arrived at the El Duede with the whole TV crew waiting. The brothers were hopeless. You never saw two such sad sacks. Not only couldn't they dance, they looked like they had never met each other before—strangers in the morning, so to speak. It was the worst performance ever filmed by anyone, living or dead.

The next Christmas, I didn't receive my usual gift from Hope. I got a lovely tin of unused film—the six hundred feet shot of my two former flamenco dancing friends.

Spiro laughed at the story and, with tears in his eyes, dismissed me with much the same wide gesture Hope had used with "the boys."

The next night we attended a black-tie function at one of New York's fanciest hotels where Agnew was the featured speaker. The Secret Service called me aside before cocktails and said the Vice President was not to eat any of the hors d'oeuvres. What a lot of people don't know is that one of the Secret Service support team is a Food and Drug man who sniffs around in the kitchen of any hotel we're in and sticks thermometers in apples, pokes them in deviled eggs, and says, "The food is unsuitable. The Vice President may not eat anything because the pate is 140 degrees." With that, Spiro avoided the buffet and hardly looked at his dinner.

Otherwise, the evening went well. Handsome speeches all around. We got back to our suite at about 11:30 and sent out for a pizza (unbeknownst to the official food sniffer) and Mr. A. turned in. I went out still dressed in my tux. I got myself into a lot of fun and crawled back at 6:00 in the morning with the responsibility of getting the man up at 7:00.

I realized the only way I could get through the wake-up was to open my shirt, take my tie off, lie down flat on the bed with my arms beside me, and breathe. Relaxing my toes and eyes, I set the clock for one hour later. When the alarm went off, I dashed some water on my face, put my black tie back on, and went into "His Excellency's" room. I threw open the draperies and said, "Good morning, sir! We have a half-hour to get ready for the black-tie breakfast."

Stunned, he sat up in bed, looked at me, and said, "The black-tie breakfast?"

"Yes, sir. You know, it's a half-hour from now." With that I went back to my room, giggling from the still-active booze.

A few minutes later, the phone buzzed and the formal voice of STA commented dryly, "There's no such thing as a black-tie breakfast."

"You figured it out, didn't you?"

We both were laughing.

"You haven't been to bed yet, have you?" he said insightfully.

The public never realized it, but Agnew was a perfect candidate for an "I Love New York" commercial. He adored the place and any semi-bona fide occasion that would take us to the Big Apple was welcomed. Be it a crippled children fund raiser or a bankers' meeting, we'd head up to Manhattan, if for no other reason than to dine in one of his two favorite restaurants: Christ Cella's (for steaks) or Patsy's (for veal and pasta).

Agnew delighted in taking long, thirty-block walks in New York, especially after a big dinner. Surrounded by the Secret Service, we'd take in Madison or Lexington avenues and work our way up to the 80's and then back to the Waldorf. These after-dinner jaunts would kill me because I prized my free time and Agnew's little strolls would considerably cut into my after-hours agenda. I used to try to get him to walk along quickly, but invariably he'd saunter, while I counted the seconds 'til I could tuck him in and head for the night life.

The Veep had ironclad patterns from which he never strayed very far. He always stopped into Countess Mara for ties; loved to browse Saks and Sulka's; and every morning I was with him in New York, he'd order up exactly the same breakfast: OJ, cranshaw melon, crisp bacon on dry English muffins, and a cup of tea. I fell into some of his patterns in New York, but I never bought quite as many ties and always added a Bloody Mary to my menu.

It was during one of those "Big Apple of Agnew's Eye" trips that Frank Sinatra joined the Vice President as a guest of honor. In Frank's entourage that weekend was a long-standing friend of his, artist and illustrator LeRoy Neiman.

Neiman hit it off quickly with Agnew and our staff. After a few afternoon cocktails, we invited him to join us that evening at the Waldorf to dine and listen to the Veep's Columbus Day speech. With Agnew and Sinatra on the dias, I invited Neiman and his assistant to sit at my table. A witty, likable man, Neiman resembled an American version of Salvador Dali, with his handlebar mustache and eccentric disposition.

Shortly after the rhetoric commenced, Neiman took out the

small 11″ × 14″ art portfolio that he always seems to have with him and started sketching. After working on a few quick studies of the honchos on the dias, he turned and started to draw what I thought was me. I decided to downplay my inner excitement over a potential Neiman portrait. I've seen these artists in action and if you alter or break their attention, they'll stop what they are doing and become self-conscious. So I sat there wondering until curiosity got the best of me and I leaned over to his assistant and whispered, "Who is he drawing?"

"Be quiet, it's you!" she whispered back. I stared at the dias without moving a muscle and without hearing a word of the speech.

With applause and a flourish, Agnew's speech ended and Neiman quickly put his drawing paper in order and zipped up his portfolio. "Well, that's that," I mused, a little disappointed. As is customary after every big dinner speech, the Vice President and company went out for a late supper. Agnew often claimed that he, like most other politicians, would merely push his food around on the plate at any of these affairs and afterward look for a good restaurant. Speech-and-dinner engagements have been nicknamed the "chicken-and-pea circuit" and you can only take so much of it.

Inviting LeRoy to join us, we headed for Patsy's, and although the artist and I had a great chat, he never did mention the drawing and I didn't have enough nerve to bring it up.

A week or so later, I received the drawing and a thoughtful thank-you note in the mail. Neiman, I was told, Xeroxes every single work of this type for his catalog before he releases it. With belated exuberance, I finally showed the others on the staff that I, too, had a personal portrait by LeRoy Neiman, just like almost everyone else I knew.

I took leave to spend Christmas in Palm Springs with my mother and father. The Agnews joined us there for a New Year's vacation, enjoying the golf, tennis, swimming, and, as always, Frank's shining hospitality. On New Year's Eve, Frank hosted a quietly festive evening, attended by those in the desert close to him, plus a few friends from Los Angeles. Ginger Rogers and her mother, generating more a feeling of family than of Hollywood, were a sentimental touch for me. Ginger was with Hope and myself during the Alaska USO tours years ago and had not forgotten those crazy shows. Even "little"

Bullets Durgan, Jackie Gleason's longtime, affable agent, showed up, accompanied by a brassy young dame who got her Oscar easier than most aspiring young stars—she took Frank's on the way out!

Two days later, Bullets, as woeful as a basset hound, returned it to an amused, but slightly miffed, Sinatra, apologizing for his souvenir-hunting girl friend's over-enthusiastic handbag.

On New Year's Day, we drove the long block to the compound of Walter Annenberg, just down the street from Frank's place. Annenberg's estate is fabulous too, in some ways grander than Frank's, but I confess I like Frank's better. Annenberg's lacked the family atmosphere of the Sinatra compound. It's tough to beat either Hope or Sinatra as hosts, but the Annenbergs tried. You can have all the luxuries, the same service, food, and every possible amenity, but without the fireside spirit it's not the same. The works of art in the Annenberg palace are of museum quality. Sinatra has fine works of art as well, but his place is still a home where you feel you can take your shoes off and lie on the couch while watching television. (And people did.) You don't get that feeling at the Annenbergs'.

In my few interactions socially with Walter and Lee Annenberg, I never got to know them well. They're aloof people and appear just this side of being downright stuffy. Walter has his own nine-hole golf course. He couldn't get the starting time he wanted at Tamarisk one Saturday, so he built his own. And it's a beauty, with two sets of tees so you can play a full eighteen holes.

Walter is extremely fussy about people taking up divots on his course, and since very few people play a clean game in that respect, things can get tense on the Annenberg nine. The day before New Year's, Spiro T., Dr. Voss, Annenberg, and I made up a foursome on Walter's turf. The Vice President did not build his career on being a tremendous golfer, but then that's not what he was getting paid to do. He had a light dip from the left shoulder when he swung and, from time to time, he'd take up a nice piece of real estate. Annenberg was twitching and I had the distinct feeling that he'd have been happier if we had gone inside and smashed some of his Steuben glassware. But at least he's prepared for the worst. Right behind us followed a man whose sole purpose in life was to replace the divots.

At one time, across the desert from the Annenbergs, about a mile away, a high-rise condominium went up. Walter was annoyed. He threw every punch he had to stop that building. Local wags said that he was sure everybody in the high-rise had field glasses focused on his bedroom, and he had plans to sell the compound because of the intrusion. Later, somebody convinced him to build a hill between the two, which he did. It destroyed part of the house's view, but his privacy was restored.

In contrast to Frank's informal soirées, most functions at the Annenbergs' are black-tie. But this New Year's Day, Walter let his hair down a bit. While we were watching the Rose Bowl game, I had the distinct impression that we were being limited to one drink. Walter made no overtures, though all our glasses were empty, so we watched the game—as did the bartender, who had nothing else to do. Finally, the Vice President asked for another. Chain reaction. We all got refills. Walter, too, decided for seconds. He leaned on the bar and spoke to his bartender in what was designed to be an aside, but became a stage whisper. "I'll have another soda water, but only if the bottle's open. Don't open a fresh one for me." Frank and I really tried not to laugh, but we were miserable failures.

That evening, the compound seemed somehow a little dull. Everyone seemed content to sit back on sofas, relax, and read. Possibly the Agnews even enjoyed *not* having anything to do for a change, but Frank and I were restless and I could see he was brewing an idea. Sinatra has a certain look that telegraphs his rambunctious moods.

While we were standing by ourselves, Frank whispered, "It's awful quiet around the compound tonight."

Ever the perfect straightman, I said, "We should stir it up a bit, huh?"

"What do you suggest?" FS grinned.

"You know," I said, "the Secret Service has really had it kind of easy this week with us here and down at Annenberg's, the other fortress. Maybe we should . . . play with them a little bit." Sinatra's grin was even broader. He was way ahead of me.

Just after dinner, as arranged, we met at the compound's old helicopter pad, which zoning ordinances now prevented Frank from using. Frank thereupon produced an enormous Mexican firecracker that he had been saving for the Fourth of July. Giggling like two school kids, Frank stuffed the almost dynamite-sized firecracker into an old lead pipe to magnify the explosion, while I devised a long fuse out of extra wicks. After we had put the bomb in place, Frank went back into the house first, and sat down in the living room to re-read the evening paper and relax with the Agnews. Figuring it would take forty-five seconds, I hid behind a bush, lit the string and ran like hell to join the others.

It had to be obvious from the way I rushed in, panting, that I was up to no good, yet the ear-busting bang even caught me by surprise. Agnew leapt to his feet. "What the hell was that?" Frank and I could only reply with a burst of laughter.

The Secret Service sprang into action, and as we gazed from the huge picture window, they seemed to be scrambling to every corner of the yard. One agent rushed into the house to protect its occupants with a fierce, nobody-move-'til-we-get-to-the-bottom-of-this look.

Others who had been combing the grounds soon came back to the house with a few broken pieces of pipe and an odd look on their faces. None of the agents directly asked me what we thought had just happened, and somewhat to my surprise, the subject was quickly dropped and the agents left the house.

While Frank and company settled back into their version of a long winter's night, I wandered outside. I knew Secret Service procedures and was mildly irked that they hadn't pursued the mystery as thoroughly as I supposed they would. I approached an agent, mumbling something about what a shock the explosion was. "Everything in the house is fine now," I said, trying to sound cooperative and reassuring. The Secret Service agent favored me with the kind of smile an indulgent parent gives a wayward child and then commented, "It does get a little dull around here. . . . We knew what you were doing before you'd got the firecracker halfway into the tube, but we decided to let you kids play." I nodded sagely, recognizing who was really having the last laugh.

Tanned, relaxed, and full of pep for the New Year, we returned to Washington. Quite aware that 1972 was, after all, an election year, we knew that our work was cut out for us. Nixon was definitely seeking reelection, but no indication of any kind had surfaced as to his intention to retain Spiro Agnew as a vice-presidential choice. In a precise move to influence that decision, Roy Goodearle, Agnew's senior political adviser and a former key Nixon aide, called a meeting with David Keene, a bright young Agnew staffer; Vic Gold; and myself. We decided on a three-fold plan. First, I was to contact John Wayne and secure his agreement to act as signer of a fundraising letter bearing the banner "Americans for Agnew." This operation was to be totally detached from our paid staff positions and would function out of California by political operatives who would be paid with funds raised by Americans for Agnew (AFA).

The funds collected from AFA were then to be used for the second political thrust: an unheard of vice-presidential write-in campaign for Agnew in the March primary in New Hampshire. The third effort was to be a superstar "Salute to Ted Agnew Night" in Baltimore. A local GOP organization in Maryland had asked to sponsor such an event, and I, with Hope and Sinatra lending a big hand, agreed to put the show together. Although Agnew was informed of this plan, he never gave it his official blessing—but neither did he squash any part of it.

The Baltimore superstar night was a spectacular affair. With Sinatra, Hope, Jimmy Stewart, Nelson Riddle, and Pat Harrington flying in on a private jet just to boost Ted Agnew, the public turnout exceeded our most optimistic predictions. It was the first time Frank had appeared since his retirement, and he attracted the national press. While the event was ostensibly a fund raiser for the Republican party of Maryland, we were really putting those stars on the line in front of the whole country as supporting the Veep.

Our strategy was, of course, to create enough fuss and furor so that it would be almost impossible for Nixon to dump Agnew, even though there was considerable gossip echoing in the halls of the White House that the President was seriously considering then-Secretary of the Treasury John B. Connally as his running mate.

Agnew's first reaction to his possible renomination was almost one of indifference. This attitude was to evolve during the next six months from nonchalance to worried annoyance and on to high anxiety.

Basically, Agnew had reason to be concerned about his renomination. He had more-or-less openly opposed Kissinger and Nixon over "Ping-Pong" diplomacy with Red China, which Agnew felt was premature. This was symptomatic of something else: During his four years in office, Agnew had become less a team player and more his own man. He often said the only reason for him to run for Veep again in 1972 was to gear up for the presidency in 1976. If Nixon chose him and he accepted, it was a signal to key staffers that all bets were on for a go at the White House.

He tossed around the unanswered question endlessly. Should he get out now and make some big bucks while he was still a hot item? But this question only ran through his mind while he remained unasked.

On the Saturday before the Super Bowl game, Mr. A. invited me over to his residence, an apartment in the Sheraton Park Hotel. I was asked to prepare a little marinara sauce, but not the same recipe I had used at my beach house in California a few years before. I always enjoyed cooking for the Agnews, but preferred to do so on my home range. This was my first "command" dinner at the boss's and I wanted to turn on my best sauce.

As I opened the cans of tomatoes, I noticed they were much more acid than usual. I reached for the phone, remembering a chat about sauces I had had with FAS and, after a little banter, asked him what he did when he had acid tomatoes. "I think you once said you used baking soda to cut it?"

Sinatra replied, "Yeah, just throw some in."

"How much?"

"Oh, throw in a couple of tablespoons."

It never dawned on me that my leg was being pulled. In a six-quart pot I tossed in what Frank recommended. The pot started to bubble and then, to my horror, erupt.

Naturally, I wasn't about to tell the ravenous Agnews that they had a semiactive volcano in their decorator kitchen. Desperately, I rummaged through the shelves looking for spices and anything else that would salvage the mess that was quickly becoming a vat of leftover Campbell's tomato soup. The great sauce that the Agnews savored and had been looking forward to all day finally emerged a sickly dish of red blandness. Nothing could save it.

We sat down to eat. Agnew tasted it, smiled, and said, "It's good . . . but it's not as good as the ones you've made before."

Of course he was being kind. It was terrible! I called Frank back the next day, but he only laughed. "You dummy! Everybody knows you only put a pinch in there. You *actually* put two tablespoons in? What the hell kind of dago cook are you?"

"Almost unemployed," I replied.

I wasn't asked to chef at the Veep's for some time. When I eventually told him about the friendly act of sabotage, he laughed. "I didn't want to tell you, 'cause I was so damn hungry, but it really was the *worst*!"

On a two-day trip to New York at the end of the month, Agnew again focused his attention on the vice-presidency. He suddenly began to express excessive and unusual solicitude for the President's peace of mind, and he emphasized that he certainly didn't want anyone on his staff to incur the displeasure of the Oval Office on his behalf. The rumors concerning Nixon's V.P. plans for Connally were rampant, and again Agnew privately voiced his utter frustration with Mr. Nixon. The few times he was able to see the President and attempted to solicit reassurance about the ticket, Agnew was never able to get a straight answer. Nixon had a great ability to command those conversations, and by the time it was over, Agnew hadn't had a chance of getting in his two cents.

In one lengthy conversation during a limo ride, Agnew commented to me, again, "Unless I have my eyes on bigger things, there's no sense in running." He continued, "I have the opportunity now to make some real money in the private sector. Who knows about the future?" He was sounding like a broken record.

That evening in the hotel, Agnew expressed his concern over the mood of the country, stating that "They [the voters] are still swinging left." Vic Gold and I disagreed with his analysis and wondered what the future held for all of us politically. The conversation ran late into the evening and afterwards I turned in. It was not an evening that warranted my usual galavanting. I had far too many things to think about.

Agnew's tense introspective mood mellowed somewhat in the warm Palm Springs weather that greeted us for the 1972 Bob Hope Desert Classic. Spiro was by now as much a fixture at the classic as he was at the Sinatra compound. This year, longtime Agnew friends from Maryland, Harry Dundore, Herb Ashcroft, and Maryland golf pro Mus Olinger, gathered at Sinatra's with the Milton Berles, the Jack Bennys, and others for a fabulous time.

Spiro managed to get through this classic without shedding innocent blood, and Palm Springs rejoiced. Inspired by this evidence that *anyone* can improve his game, Sinatra, Danny Schwartz, and I decided to give our swings a try at Tamarisk Country Club. It was an unusually hot day for that time of year in the Springs, and nine holes were more than enough. We stopped at the club bar for "just one drink." Many Stolichnayas later, Frank and I left the clubhouse and I commented aloud, "I can't wait to get into the pool. Let's hurry."

Apparently, Frank agreed. He quickly maneuvered the cart through the rear gates of the compound off the eighth hole, across the surrounding grounds, past his lounging guests, and directly into the deep end of the swimming pool. Berle, Benny, Agnew, and everyone around the pool looked up from their sunbathing and politely gave us a small hand.

As I surfaced three seconds later, I heard old "smooth voice" asking me, "Was that fast enough?"

"Perfect! But I was hoping I'd be able to take my shoes off first!"

The remainder of the week was passed in parties, golf, and good times, culminating with Frank's birthday fest for Benny. Jack had to be one of the first five of the most loved performers ever in Hollywood. His marvelous humor and style encompassed every part of his being. His warmth, friendliness, and startling humility were inspiring.

Throughout the years, I never heard Bob Hope speak ill of anyone in show business. If he didn't care for somebody's act, it remained a secret known only to him. (He was no Sinatra in that respect.) But those close to Hope would always spot a special kind of reaction if he really admired another performer. This was never more obvious than in the case of Jack Benny.

Whenever Hope saw Benny on television or stage, he'd laugh a bit louder than usual, shake his head, and mumble, "Isn't he great! He's just the greatest!" Whenever Benny's name came up, Hope always spoke of him with the deepest warmth, and it was obvious that he held Benny in as high regard as anyone in show business.

It isn't difficult to understand why. Benny, despite all his success and wealth, still possessed a shy charm that bordered on embarrassment when he was the subject of adulation. At the same time, he was marvelously outgoing. He treated his new friends, Agnew and company, with the same enthusiasm he gave his old ones.

We returned to Washington in time to see President Nixon depart on his historic trip to China. The Veep remained in the Capital, as he always did when the President was out of the country. In preparation for Nixon's return, Bob Haldeman called Art Sohmer and informed him that the President was arriving at Andrews Air Force Base on February 28 and that he would like the Vice President "to welcome him back and speak for three minutes." Agnew was to be part of an orchestrated White House extravaganza. Returning home, Richard Nixon would deplane in glory. Spiro Agnew now openly admitted that the trip to China had been an unexpected success. He publicly admired Nixon for taking the step toward re-opening the door between the two nations, even though he continued to be privately skeptical and insisted to his staff that he still felt the trip was premature. Nevertheless, the triumphant return of Nixon warranted that he write this speech himself.

When the presidential plane landed, there was much fanfare: ruffles and flourishes; honor guards; the Cabinet; and every big wheel in the administration were on hand. The plane pulled into the hangar. Before Nixon unboarded, the Vice President, addressing a throng of thousands, hailed Nixon's achievement in China and then went on to list a few more accomplishments of the President. He got carried away, continuing for considerably more than the prescribed three minutes. I was in the rear of the hangar.

Haldeman caught my eye, grabbed me by the arm, and said, "I told Art that the Vice President was to have *three* minutes. He's been on for nine!"

I said, "Well, Bob, we go back a long time, but there are a few things I've never been able to figure out. One is why this kind of thing bothers you. You're right. The Vice President has spoken for more than his granted three minutes. So what? And why bitch at me? If you've got something to say to him, you get off your ass and go tell him yourself. As far as I'm concerned, either you or one of your go-fers can tell him to stop talking, but I'm certainly not going to do it."

Bob was flabbergasted. Sternly, with a clenched jaw, he said, "I want him *off*!"

At that, I lost what little cool I had. "You know, Bob," I shouted, "I am really tired of your bullshit. If you want him off, you can walk up to the podium, you can tap him on the shoulder, and you can say, 'Pal, the President says your three minutes are up!' But short of that, Bob, you can *get off my ass*!"

With that, I walked away and the dignified crowd around us went bananas. The two of us must have made quite a picture. It was always Haldeman's role to be a power-by-proxy: "The President wants this. The President wants that." It was the one way of addressing information to Mr. Agnew that irritated him most, and Haldeman was famous for it.

Once again the issue of the Gridiron Dinner came up at the White House. As usual, it was Haldeman who called our office. Only on the rarest of occasions did Richard Nixon communicate directly with the Vice President. H. R. Haldeman was, in effect, the official channel of communications.

"The President would like Mr. Agnew to do the Gridiron Dinner again," Haldeman told Art Sohmer.

Hearing this from Art, I spoke to the Vice President. He was not amused: "I filled in last year. They really want the President."

Mr. Agnew always held a higher vision of the power of the presidency than I. But though he'd always arrange his schedule to accommodate Nixon, he couldn't help being irked by the chain of command used by the President.

"Did Mr. Nixon himself call me on this?"

"No, sir, it was Mr. Haldeman."

"Well, Peter, that doesn't count much. I'm not sure how to approach this."

I reminded him that somebody or other had invited him to speak in New Orleans on that date, and that the staff had accepted for him. "We won't be here for it, sir."

"Do you think we can get away with that?" he asked.

"Indeed we will, Mr. Agnew."

I called John Damgard in the scheduling office and asked him to confirm the Vice President into New Orleans for four days—quickly! We got to the hotel on Saturday, with the Gridiron Dinner approaching on the following Tuesday. We knew the President was serious about not attending the dinner himself, but, to my surprise, a call came in from Procter & Gamble's man Bryce Harlow, a respected presidential adviser and a man of whom Agnew thought the world.

After exchanging greetings with me, Bryce got right to the point. "The President is concerned about the Gridiron thing coming up, and he's very firm about the Vice President filling in for him."

"Bryce," I replied, "it may be important to the President, but it is equally important to Mr. Agnew that he speak before this crowd in New Orleans. Mr. Agnew is thoroughly committed here."

Bryce asked, "I'd like to speak to the Vice President."

"Right away, Bryce," I told him as I put him on hold. "Mr. Agnew, Mr. Harlow is on the phone," I said.

"What's the matter?"

"He's calling about the damn Gridiron Dinner."

Agnew's exchange with Harlow was pleasant but simple. It was agreed that the Vice President would be unable to attend the dinner, and that was that.

The next day, at two o'clock, we received an urgent message from the White House communications center informing us that a military courier, a major general in fact, was en route with an important message for the Vice President. The general was being personally flown down in a presidential jet, and the center wanted to know exactly where Mr. Agnew was going to be at 8:30 P.M. I relayed the information to Spiro T. and he was quite taken aback. "This must be terribly important. I'll be wherever they want."

I returned the call to Washington, stating we would be in the suite at the appointed time. The White House staff coordinated the jet to arrive at 7:30 P.M., with immediate limousine service for the general. I was thinking, "I wonder if it's all over. Maybe the bomb goes off at noon tomorrow." The urgency of the plane flight was ominous, to say the least.

Still, knowing Mr. Nixon, my suspicions returned to the Gridiron Dinner. I was almost sure that this was some device to shake up Agnew. I said, "Mr. Vice President, I suspect this whole charade is an effort to get you to speak at the Gridiron affair."

"Nonsense!" Agnew responded firmly. "Peter, this is very serious business. When the President dispatches a courier with a handwritten note, it couldn't possibly be that trivial."

I said, "If that's the case, may I have the handwritten note against two bottles of Chivas Regal?"

"You've got a deal."

The courier arrived on time and knocked on the door of the suite. He said, "I have a message from the President of the United States for the Vice President."

"Fine," I said with my hand out. "Give me the note."

"No, sir! This must be delivered personally."

"Look," I retorted with feigned exasperation, "he's sitting right there. Give me the note. You can watch me hand it to him." I took it and handed the impressive linen-paper envelope to the Vice President. I smiled, "Is our bet still on?"

"Just open the goddamn envelope," Agnew snapped, "and read it! No dialogue."

The letter turned out to be almost exactly what I had expected. It seemed that the President was filled with sympathy and solicitude for all the many ceremonial duties the Vice President was called upon to discharge. After all, when he had, himself, served in the same capacity under Ike . . . blah, blah, blah. Nevertheless, with respect to the Gridiron Dinner, he felt he had no alternative but to ask that the Vice President . . . blah, blah, blah. The letter was signed "Dick."

Agnew's eyes hit the ceiling. "Why the hell didn't he ask me? Why the hell didn't he just pick up the phone and say, 'Ted, will you do this for me?' No, I had to mess around with Harlow, Haldeman, and military go-fers. I will never understand the way he does things, Peter."

"Well, I said, "that's the kind of man he is."

Agnew did the dinner the next night.

We spent another memorable weekend together in Palm Springs during Easter 1972. Frank was entertaining Prince Rainier and his family. Grace's relationship with Frank goes back many years, and they share a *High Society* kinship that is a joy to witness. Equally pleasant to watch was the way Grace behaved with her charming youngsters, with whom she was as loving, strict, and concerned as any American mother raising her flock. Even though there are not many places to run off to in Palm Springs, she always wanted to know where the kids were and what they were doing. It was never left up to the governesses; Grace was always there.

After one of Frank's cinema soirées, he put on some dancing music and rolled up the rug. I danced with Caroline, Albie danced with his mother, and Frank did a few steps with little Stephanie. It was a very relaxed time, but nevertheless, when the hour was up, first Stephanie was sent to bed, then Albie, then Caroline, all in order of their ages. Naturally, the kids would always do a little P.R. number to stay up a bit longer, but Grace raised her eyes, spoke in a soft voice, and off they went. One night, they granted Albie a small extension and, with royal approval, allowed him to sit at the bar and have a beer with Frank and "the boys." A treat, even for a prince.

Albie made quite an impression. He's bright and it shows. At the time, there was discussion about which college he should attend. His family finally decided on Amherst, where, I've heard, he's done quite well. Caroline was still a raven-eyed teenager, with all the promise of someday being a ravishing beauty, not yet in the social whirlwind she seems to enjoy so much now. Stephanie? Stephanie just wanted to know when the Easter egg hunt was going to start.

This was my first informal encounter with Princess Grace and her family, although we certainly kept popping up in each other's lives in Washington, Monte Carlo, Iran, and again in Washington. There was not a shred of pretentiousness in any of the members of this family. They were family guests at Sinatra's and they behaved that way. Prince Rainier at first seemed a little aloof, but I soon concluded that this was mainly shyness. Perhaps Palm Springs casual was a bit foreign to him. He was responsive to all the antics of Sinatra and his friends, but there was always a hint of reserve. Grace extended herself with more sparkle, but then I suppose that neither of them will ever be accused of being over-animated.

Whatever initial reservations I may have had about Rainier were dispelled on the second day, when he and I took in nine holes of golf to pass the afternoon. With just the two of us in the golf cart, I found him a quick-witted, lively person. We shared recollections about Frank's escapades in Monte Carlo and the way the singer would openly discuss his candid impressions of other celebrities. The prince and I fooled around on the green like a couple of sophomores. By the end of our golf set, I was enjoying my own risqué jokes all over again, because he responded so vivaciously. He has a hearty laugh and it's catchy.

Momma Sinatra was everybody's mother. Yet, Dolly Sinatra was also a tough Italian lady who lived her own life. As close as she was to her son and grandchildren, she was still independent of Frank. She had her own home and her own circle of friends, and, when necessary, her own choice words.

Once, a few days before Mother's Day, I was enjoying the weekend off as a guest of Frank's in New York, where he maintained a suite at the Waldorf Towers. Frank said, "Mom, Mother's Day is Sunday. What do you want?"

"Oh, Frank, I don't want anything. You've given me everything already. What do I need?" She acted almost annoyed.

"Ah, c'mon Mom, there must be something you want," he pleaded.

"Ah, stop the crap, Frank. I don't need anything." When Frank pressed her for a third time, she said, "All right! You wanna give me something. Give me Cary Grant!"

We all laughed. Probably every mother in the country would like to have Cary Grant on her doorstep on Mother's Day.

The next Sunday we all went as Frank's guests for a Mother's Day dinner at Patsy's, a superb Italian restaurant with a quiet upstairs room on the West Side of Manhattan. Our group included Frank, Momma, Barbara Marx, Jilly Rizzo, and myself, plus a few of the usual groupies who surrounded Frank and Jilly in New York. Frank seated everyone at the table. No matter where or when you had dinner with Frank, whether it was twenty people or four, he automatically assumed the posture of a host and you waited to be seated.

He put himself at the head of the table, his mother to his right, Barbara to his left. The rest of the gang filled out the table. The dinner was pre-ordered, and by the time we all had a drink, the first course was being served.

Then, up the stairs and into the room sauntered the one and only Cary Grant. He arrived while Momma's head was turned, and Frank said, "Oh, by the way, Mom, here's your present."

"Hi, Momma," said Cary, planting a gentle kiss on her flushed cheek.

"Sit down," she chirped. "I wanna talk to you! You're my favorite!" The dear lady then spent the next fifteen minutes locked in visual embrace with her Mother's Day present. They held hands and quickly became friends while their dinners got cold and the rest of us pretended we weren't watching.

Cary Grant was Cary Grant—charming.

"How's your mother?" Momma asked, mindful that Cary's mother was still alive. Pleasantly taken aback, Cary explained how she was doing well and had just passed into her nineties with flying colors!

"Oh, God bless her!" Momma beamed. "And what's *she* doing today?" Cary, always a diplomat, gently explained that as wonderful as mothers are, there was no such special day in England.

Later on, Cary and I had a brisk chat. He had just kicked the smoking habit. I was smoking more and definitely enjoying it less. Cary proceeded to explain to me how effective his hypnotist was in helping him quit. For a year afterward, we had a running joke about cigarettes. He got a kick out of phoning me unannounced at the White House and mimicking his own classic line: "Petah, Petah, Petah . . . when are you going to stop smoking?"

I found myself in New York later that same month with the Vice President. Agnew was very quiet with me one afternoon. He said, "There's a man coming up for cocktails at five o'clock. I don't want his name known. Clear him through the desk and Secret Service without any fanfare."

"What is his name so I can clear him?"

"I don't want his name known!"

"I know that, but what am I going to say . . . 'An unknown man is coming to see the Veep,' sir?"

"Alright, it's Mr. Onassis."

"*The* Onassis?"

"Yes."

I went down to the desk at the Waldorf Towers and arranged for a discreet elevator. As it happened, our guest arrived at about 4:45 for the 5:00 appointment. The Vice President was in conference with another person. So I sat down with Onassis, this small tycoon and giant world power. He said to me, as we chatted in the suite, "Ma-la-tes-ta . . . Malatesta . . . My dearest boyhood friend was named Malatesta. This man has been a friend of mine for years." Then he grinned. "You know what it means, Malatesta? Sick in the head; a headache."

We chatted about the Malatestas and our backgrounds until the Vice President entered and I took my leave. To this day, I do not know what the two discussed.

That night, after the Vice President had retired, I went to one of my favorite joints, El Morocco, with a few staff members and their girl friends. No sooner were we seated than two bottles of Dom Perignon came over and the waiter said, "Mr. Malatesta. Compliments of Mr. Onassis."

It goes without saying, there are few more impressive things to do at El Morocco than to have a bottle or two of Dom Perignon sent over to your table by good old Ari. If that doesn't enhance your reputation, nothing will. I decided to make the most of it. I turned around and saw him buried in the corner, surrounded by other people. I walked over, and he said, "Malatesta! *Come sta?*"

"*Bene, bene!* Come and meet my friends!"

For the next two hours, I bounced between the tables while Onassis told his friends of his affinity for my name and I told my friends the circumstances behind our pleasant meeting. Late into the evening, with his arm raised high, Ari said, "The name Malatesta will always be welcome in the house of Onassis."

I don't know about that, but certainly the name Malatesta became suddenly welcome to Angelo, the maitre d' at El Morocco, who at once affixed a "good table" notation to it. That depressed me a bit: My customary conservative gratuity would no longer be sufficient.

On June 16, two days after my meeting with Ari, I was invited to an ambassadorial garden reception in Washington. There I ran into John Mitchell, with whom I enjoyed a pleasant rapport. John was the only senior member of the Nixon inner sanctum who was consistently civil, if not cheerful, with me.

Chatting at the bar, our conversation naturally drifted to the question of Agnew's being on the ticket. Almost immediately, Mitchell deflected the topic, saying, "I'll talk to you in a few minutes." He then wandered off by himself, away from the party, to the far reaches of the surrounding gardens. He stood under a huge oak tree and lit his ever-present pipe.

I walked over and smiled nervously. He knew what was on my mind, because it was on everybody's mind. He put his hand on my shoulder and said simply, "You've got nothing to worry about."

"I might have, John. I may have to go out and get a job back in the real world."

"No. All you've got to worry about is whether Agnew will keep you on his staff."

"You mean it's all set?"

He laughed. "Let me put it to you this way. Agnew's got nothing to worry about."

That evening, I reported posthaste to Agnew. In my mind, I was totally convinced the Vice President was going to be on the ticket. In spite of my optimism, Agnew remained uncertain. "John was just saying that to be nice to you," he sighed.

"No way! Mitchell and I don't have that kind of relationship. He's not going to stand there under an oak tree and kid to my face. He would have skirted the conversation totally. You know John!"

But Agnew merely shrugged.

The first thing the next morning, Agnew phoned me. He had mulled it over and now he said, "Peter, have them write me a swan song." Then he added lightheartedly, "And while you're at it, write me an acceptance speech."

The Fourth of July weekend was upon us and the staff was disintegrating. While most of them eagerly packed picnics for a day in the park or planned a few days in Ocean City, I was busy securing my reservations to London to rendezvous with Frank Sinatra and Vic Damone, who were waiting with a private jet to carry us all to Monte Carlo.

I still remember the Heathrow Airport stop-over because it was the first time the Concorde SST was landing in Great Britain and my commercial flight was delayed. When I finally got to Monaco, I found that Sinatra had chartered a private yacht. We sailed to Nice on sunny seas, singing over salmon and champagne. Barbara Marx, now a constant companion, was with Frank and the yacht provided us as pleasant a way as any to pick up Tina Sinatra and a girl friend, who were waiting on the dock.

Despite our pleasant surroundings, Frank was in an unusually pensive mood and far from talkative. He had a hacking cough and was often grouchy. He hinted that he might be coming out of retirement, but it wasn't spoken with excitement or anticipation. The year before, during the same period, Frank was estimated to have spent approximately $10,000 a day, a figure which his attorney, Mickey Rudin, mentioned to me during the course of a conversation. I was told Sinatra had an allowance of $2 million a year. Thanks to his savings and investments, Frank could have spent more, but $3.6 million was pushing things. As Mickey told me, "If he's going to spend that kind of money, he's going to have to go to work again."

On the Fourth of July, Frank decided a celebration was in order. He arranged for a party at Jimmy's and sent his chauffeur down to Nice with $500, specifically to fill a station wagon full of fireworks. The site of Jimmy's, an open-air disco on a lagoon, was perfect for what Frank wanted to do. We propped up an American flag on our table and, with a little help from Jack Daniels and Dom Perignon, sang our American songs. Frank hired some kids to sing and dance, and the grand finale was a thirty-minute explosion of red, white, and blue over the water.

"No way we're letting the Fourth go by without acknowledging our independence," Frank declared. And independent we were. Surrounded by some of Europe's haughtiest jetsetters, we made a brassy and robust American presence.

With the exception of the Fourth at Jimmy's, we spent a relatively quiet time. We were so self-contained that even Frank had no idea why Damone had suddenly disappeared one afternoon. We wrote it off as "space time" and made little mention of it until Vic reappeared in the early evening, exuberantly inviting us to his room, which he had "redecorated."

It seems that Damone had decided to tackle the munchies and

had slipped across the border into Italy, where he loaded up on cheeses, peppers, long loaves of bread, proscuitto, pastries, and salamis, which now hung festooned throughout his suite. It had to be the Riviera's fanciest deli and in the following days we gathered there often for sandwiches and wine rather than face the oglers on the street.

When my short weekend ended, I prepared to make my return trip on a commercial flight. Frank had provided me with his limo and chauffeur for the ride to the airport in Nice, and I had slipped the driver a few bucks to fetch some fireworks, just as he had done for Frank a few days before.

Leaving the Hotel de Paris very early in the morning, I looked up at Frank and Vic's suites on the second floor, overlooking the entrance. Then I put a match to five or six strings of blockbusting firecrackers below their balconies and laughed as they rushed to the windows, sleepy-eyed.

"*Arrivederci! . . . Grazie!*" I bellowed, as they waved in the morning sun.

A week later, as we traveled to the airport for a flight to Houston, Agnew broke into my still-euphoric holiday bubble. "I got a call from the President's office," he said sternly, "and they asked me who you were working for—me or Sinatra? Peter, they saw that picture of you and Frank taken over the Fourth."

"What picture are you talking about?"

"I suggest you buy today's copy of *Life* and go on a diet," he said wryly.

I rushed to the airport newsstand. There it was, Sinatra, Barbara, and myself in lounge chairs. I looked like an overstuffed Aga Khan. Lest anyone miss the point, I was clearly identified as "Vice Presidential Aide Peter J. Malatesta." The large, two-page spread and accompanying text reeked of intrigue and luxury. Decidedly not the type of image Nixonian Washington expected from a lowly Veep assistant.

All I could think of to say was, "What the hell, sir! At least they spelled the name right."

A week later, Frank flew into Washington to testify before the House Select Committee on Crime, investigating his alleged underworld connections. Two nights before Frank's day in court, Nick Ruwe, Nixon's assistant chief of protocol, and I threw a poolside stag party for him at Nick's house. The bash didn't fully break up until 5:00 A.M. Although there was no press present, the morning gossip mill greatly exaggerated the evening's goings-on, almost to the point of scandal. The White House got wind of it early, since a half-dozen middle-to-senior level staffers were present. While Sinatra, Ruwe, and myself were bachelors, many of the other guests were not. And not surprisingly, it was the married ones who were the friskiest. As Nick said gloomily later, the filters of the pool were never the same.

But 1600 Pennsylvania Avenue and Agnew's office were angry. I was summoned by Agnew himself early Saturday morning and was grilled on my judgment in allowing so many prominent people to be compromised at such a party. I reminded Agnew that Sinatra had left early, prior to any shenanigans, and that the party was not held at my house. I added that everyone invited was over the age of twenty-one—"The guys, anyway!" But even though I insisted that the poolside capers had been blown way out of proportion, Agnew still looked down his long beak with disbelieving annoyance. The conversation did not last much longer than that.

I left Agnew's office with a roaring headache and the realization that my position had eroded considerably over the last three weeks.

I was again summoned on Monday, this time by Sinatra. After having earlier consulted with Agnew, he had now scheduled a meeting at the Madison Hotel with Mickey Rudin, Vic Gold, and myself. For the better part of three hours, we discussed the approach Sinatra would take. "Low-keyed" was the continual catch-phrase. Frank listened thoughtfully to our presentation and nodded approvingly to our suggestion that he proceed calmly.

But it would require all his self-control. Dining with Agnew that evening, Frank was steaming over the press. "Why can't they ever tell the good side?" he kept repeating. He was hypersensitive about these press attacks, claiming they were after him because "my name ends in a vowel." Despairing over his inability to retaliate, Frank was livid.

The next morning, Sinatra was at his best. He went in with gut instincts and blew the committee members apart. Calling them "indecent and irresponsible," he chastised them for permitting an admitted murderer, Joseph Barboza, to testify against him. He then cooled down and efficiently denied all allegations.

Afterwards, ABC's Sam Donaldson chased after Sinatra and Rudin and gave them one of those "When did you stop beating your wife?" questions about Mafia involvement. Rudin quickly ended that by cracking to Donaldson, "I hear you're a homosexual." Completely unfounded, of course, but so were the charges against Frank. It was a theatrical way to leave the hearing room.

Three days after the smoke from the hearing had cleared, Spiro had some news of his own to make. He called a full staff meeting at 3:30 P.M. and said, "The President wants me."

At this time, Agnew's stock was soaring. Early in the following month, Agnew, Sinatra, Governor Reagan, and I played golf in California. The conversation transcended the 1972 election, long taken for granted. Positions were being jockeyed for what role each of us was to play in Agnew's 1976 bid for the presidency and how to best approach that goal. Having both been governors, Reagan and Agnew were no strangers, and Reagan was ready to play ball with Agnew's team, at least in an advisory capacity.

After the game, Eva Gabor hosted a party at her beach house for the Vice President, and the turnout was a who's-who of Hollywood. The support Agnew was garnering in the entertainment industry was staggering.

Eva's party was a golden opportunity for Agnew to meet face-to-face hitherto uncommitted stars. While many of them had serious reservations bordering on disdain for Richard Nixon, they all seemed open to Agnew's candor and straightforwardness.

Spiro's strongest shot was the personable impression he created with people in his first face-to-face meeting with them. These celebrities, like the rest of us, are inclined to pass judgment based on initial contact. Follow-up phone calls and letters also play a part, but nothing can top the spontaneous social combustion of a good first impression, especially at a party like this.

Striking while the iron was hot, I lined up a tennis match between Tony Quinn and the Veep, another one between him and Chuck Heston, and a luncheon with Suzanne Pleshette. I also made sure that he and Peter Falk had a chance to chat and nudged him to be attentive during one of Zsa Zsa's run-on adventures.

I remember asking Johnny Carson if he wanted to meet the Vice President. Johnny had been standing in a corner with his hands in his pockets. With a shy grin, he agreed, but only after considerable hemming and hawing. Even then, I had to bring Agnew over to the corner to meet the gregarious TV host. They ended up enjoying an animated half-hour conversation. Sinatra decided to announce publicly for Nixon-Agnew the next day.

The Republican Convention of 1972 in Miami held few surprises. Perhaps the most exciting moments were its social aspects. Certainly, the high visibility of entertainers like Sinatra and John Wayne were "items" most Republican delegates had not experienced.

The night before the nomination, Sinatra, Wayne, and I headed over to the Playboy Club to tip a few for our man. I never had had the chance to sit down informally and drink eye-to-eye with the legendary Duke. He was full of salty tales about his career and his close friendship with Frank, who'd laugh and come back with a few yarns of his own. Later, we were joined by comedian Jerry Lester, actress Ruta Lee, and impersonator David Frye, who rounded out the table and added even more zest.

The convention setting brought out the public side of Sinatra. When Frank decides he's going to go out and do something—even though he's a relative newcomer, as at the GOP convention—he can be brilliant at it. Patting backs, greeting strangers, and accommodating autograph-seekers, Sinatra can treat everyone like his good pal if he's so inclined.

As tradition demands, Agnew first set foot in the convention the night of his actual nomination. Agnew and I were alone in the holding room under the podium and he was visibly charged and genuinely happy. Looking like a scrubbed baby, his face was aglow. Immediately after the vote was taken confirming his nomination, he put his arm around me and said, "I never thought we'd get it this way."

This was Agnew's finest moment. But Watergate, or at least the break-in, was already history-in-the-making, and little did we know that thirteen and a half months later Agnew would precede the Watergate scandal into a disgrace of his own.

The campaign kicked off in September. It was an unrockable boat. The polls consistently showed us ahead, and the crowds never failed to appear. Of all the presidential campaigns I've worked on, this was the smoothest. Agnew delivered his speeches eloquently and often wrote them himself. He was no longer the baiter of the elite, nor did he appear in the shadow of Richard Nixon, and he used the campaign diligently to advance his claim on a paramount role in 1976.

The course of the vote-gathering effort often became tedious and mechanical. Although I took my position in government seriously, I've never had a high threshold for boredom, and I confess that after a while the monotony of the campaign was beginning to get me down a little. I began thinking about my own future. I liked what Perle Mesta had told me and I liked the first party I had hosted for Frank. Lying awake in countless hotel rooms, I started to reflect upon a positive course that would steer me into my own orbit socially and financially.

I couldn't face a future of just being an aide, even though that role had taken me on a first-class ride to the four corners of the globe. While the sensation of high-profile traveling offered many varied rewards, it could also leave me depressed and lonely, especially if the trip was, as usual, "rush, rush, rush!" Often my sense of humor was my only umbilical cord to normalcy.

We were faced with a typically hectic agenda upon landing in San Diego. We had approximately twenty-five minutes to get to our hotel and change before heading to the next scheduled function. Spiro turned to me in the car and said, "You know, Peter, I'm hungry!"

"Why don't we stop at the next Jack-in-the-Box?" I replied, intending a little tired irony.

"What?"

"Jack-in-the-Box! Every place has a Jack-in-the-Box!"

Spiro became very serious. "It's a hamburger joint, isn't it? I saw it on television. I want to eat there."

I called the lead car and said to the Secret Service, "The next Jack-in-the-Box we come to, drive through. The Vice President wants a hamburger."

The agent in the lead car sounded baffled. "I beg your pardon?"

I laughed. "Don't beg my pardon. Just stop in the next Jack-in-the-Box. We wanna eat."

It wasn't more than a mile down the road when we came to one on the right-hand side. In went the lead car, which is always the police car of the State; the second car, which is the local police; the third car, a Secret Service vehicle; the fourth, the vice-presidential limousine;

the fifth, the Secret Service station wagon, full of heavier weapons; followed by a sixth car used by the communications people; followed by two more cars with staff and press.

Eight cars, but no one in them knew what to do or what to order, because we came upon the Jack-in-the-Box so quickly. The lead car stopped at the little window and radioed back, "What shall we do now?"

Agnew's reply over the limo radio was stern: "Count up the people and order the hamburgers."

The cop looked up at the young lady in the window and said, "Thirty-two hamburgers to go."

One by one, each car stopped and picked up their bag, while the people inside the take-out ogled until it hurt.

We campaigned right up to 11:00 P.M. on election eve and spent the rest of the night at the Shoreham Hotel with Sinatra and several of the Vice President's Maryland cronies, including Bud Hammerman and J. Walter Jones. Later, Hammerman's testimony against his pal Spiro would be crucial.

The networks declared the Nixon-Agnew ticket as the winners even before the California polls closed, so whatever glow that comes with victory seemed anticlimactic. It seemed to me that this election had had all the excitement of Oscar night the year *Gone With the Wind* swept away everything.

The balance of the year was spent on R and R, with Agnew traveling to the Virgin Islands. In late November, we made a trip to Palm Springs, and Frank and I talked about the next four years and, more importantly, the four years after that. Sinatra was now determined to see an Agnew presidency. In fact, he went on record in the press as saying he "would make Agnew President." But I was of two minds. I saw four more years as a staffer, rat-racing between Nixon and Agnew. Beyond that, if Agnew were to go on to better things, probably the best I could hope for would be to be appointed consul-general to the Bahamas. And what would I do after that?

Frank's visions were known only to him, but he stressed this point during our lengthy conversation. "Stick with the old man. He needs you. If he doesn't take good care of you, I will." By the end of the evening, Frank asked me to find a suitable house that we could share in Washington during our forthcoming years. He realized he'd be spending a great deal more time there, and it was advantageous, from an economic and personal viewpoint, to lease a house. He needed a base to showcase Agnew for the presidency. Sinatra felt like a kingmaker and a kingmaker needs a castle.

I had been working Sinatra for months to take a place of our own and now he had finally come up with the idea. I was to be in on the ground floor of what could be the hottest new act in Washington: Sinatra as a part-time host on Embassy Row and Malatesta as a full-time one. Our castle would be the vehicle which would propel my identity from that of a mere aide to that of a socialite. It might have been a side-door entrance, but I felt sure it would work. I ordered another three dozen hand towels; two dozen embroidered with "PM" and a dozen with "FS."

Chapter Six

My favorite pad in Washington belonged to my friend Virginia Page, who had entertained Chuck Connors and me so royally there during the 1969 inauguration. It was a beige, California-style brick house on 24th Street, a shady tree-lined lane off Embassy Row. While not huge, it was a large, comfortable home with connecting twin living rooms, five bedrooms, marble flooring, four fireplaces, and thick, brick walls surrounding the pool. Its circular driveway allowed for quick, Sinatra-style exits, and its marble wet bar was ready to serve up party politics on the rocks.

Leasing the place couldn't have been easier. Virginia had just said good-bye to tenant Tongsun Park, a Korean businessman, who had started his rise to social power by buying considerably more formal digs nearby. Viscountess Gertrude D'Amecourt, a fashionable Embassy Row realtor, handled the property and she couldn't have been more helpful. Gertie, like Virginia Page, had taken me under her wing and given me my first taste of Embassy Row parties. She told me that the elegant $2,000-a-month house on 24th Street would be available in a matter of weeks.

Frank was in Washington at the time, and moments after calling D'Amecourt we limoed over for a look, parking the car a half a block away because gossip spreads faster in D.C. than it does in a sorority house and we wanted our house-hunting to be as low-profile as possible. Frank loved the place and took it with a year's lease on the spot.

I no sooner got back to my office at the White House when the phone rang. It was *Washington Star* society columnist Betty Beale wanting to know if Frank and I were renting Page's house on 24th Street. I hadn't been at my desk for five minutes and it flabbergasted me how quickly the word traveled. It seems that right across the street from our new place there lived a lady who, apparently, was consumed with curiosity about the new tenants. Mrs. Endicott Peabody, the wife of a former governor of Massachusetts, was the lady in question, and we would soon become accustomed to seeing her in the upstairs window of her home, watching us like a hawk whenever we were preparing to have a party. For more than a year, Frank and I gave her an eyeful.

With inaugural week at hand, we went to W & J Sloane Inc. and Frank bought, off the floor, anything and everything he saw that would complement the house. By the time the smoke cleared that afternoon, he had bought sofas, tables, a piano, lamps—all things to add to an already well-furnished home. Like everything else in his life, the house had to bear the Sinatra touch. He bought Oriental rugs, wall hangings, and such, but all on one condition: All of it had to be delivered the *next* afternoon, because we were entertaining that night. He charmed the hell out of the saleswoman and gave her an extra hundred bucks for her trouble. Sure enough, everything was in place by 4:30 P.M. the next day. At 8:00, we received our first guests.

Frank cut a deal with his liquor-distributing friends, and biweekly deliveries of Cutty Sark, Dom Perignon, Jack Daniels Black, and Michelob on tap filled our storeroom. We were ready for a wet winter.

Our big inauguration bash was actually a series of several politically oriented parties. Frank used the affairs to bore into the upper-level bureaucratic woodwork, while I chose to use the parties to try to improve my social standing. Frank had it made, but I was just preparing to splash onto Washington's social pages. Still, the house was a setup over which most social climbers would fantasize.

With Spiro and Judy Agnew topping the guest list, Sinatra and I welcomed Henry Kissinger, his parents, and then-steady companion Nancy McGinnis; Eva Gabor; senators Barry Goldwater and John Tower; John and Martha Mitchell; Ambassador and Mrs. John Volpe; and Anna Chennault. Standing in the grand foyer under a baccarat chandelier, Kissinger said dryly, "Peter, this is unfair! *I* belong in this house. You should be around the corner in my little place."

As the days rolled on, the parties continued with a momentum that fascinated the local press. We entertained Alan Shepard, Sammy Davis, Jr., Jack Valenti, Pat Boone, Mary Ann Mobley, Mike Curb, and the ambassadors of Italy, Saudi Arabia, Tunisia, and Morocco.

On inaugural eve, Frank was truly at his best. During our entire association, I never heard Frank sing at a party, except on this particular evening. (If guests were lucky, he'd hum to the music but Sinatra was never keen on performing privately.) We started about midnight and served omelettes and Dom Perignon. Frank had invited an old friend, Monty Alexander, a superb jazz pianist who happened to be playing at Blues Alley, a local jazz club. As Monty tinkered away, his playing attracted another guest, Vikki Carr, who softly slid into a few songs as she stood listening to him. Once Vikki started, the seating area near the piano filled up quickly—floor and all! Frank chose a comfortable spot on the rug near the piano and pleasantly sipped his Jack Daniels and hummed a little while Carr increased her impromptu songs into a cozy performance, lasting a good forty-five minutes.

As Monty continued to play seductively, Sinatra started to sing without any real cue. Still sitting with his shoulders against the wall, drink in hand, Frank never sounded better. I was amazed; singing through a medley of classics, he held the room spellbound. No one moved except to signal shyly to a waiter for a refill. Kissinger seemed almost speechless, which I construed to be a first of sorts. And so the night slipped away, with no one budging from the living room floor until 5:00 A.M.

These first parties were groundwork events. Most of the guests held sensitive upper-level government and corporate positions, and no one was so naive as to be willing to discuss any matters of substance at this early stage. Testing the social waters involves meticulous attention to timing. Obviously, anyone charging up to an Arab ambassador on a first meeting with the equivalent of "Have I got an arms deal for you!" is going to find himself an unwelcome intruder at future parties and a lonesome host at home.

Our inauguration galas sparkled with success, and Frank felt increasingly comfortable in the Capital. One incident on inauguration night, however, almost ruined our good start.

Frank, Barbara, and I were chatting over lunch at the house. Frank had been very active in the campaign, and it was logical that he should attend a private bash being given that evening by the Republican finance committee and hosted by Louise Gore at the Jockey Club. Frank wasn't sure he wanted to go, but I said, "Frank, I know you hate this kind of affair, but 'everyone' is going to be there! Why don't we just drop by for a few minutes and say hello?" If Sinatra was going to score a few points with this administration, Gore's party was the right ball game.

We arrived at the Jockey Club to a line of photographers and a battery of press, among them Maxine Cheshire covering gossip for *The Washington Post*. Relations between Frank and Maxine had been strained ever since a run-in they had at the yearly Governors' Ball several months before.

So it wasn't surprising that her first question was abrupt and barbed. "What does the Vice President think of your Mafia connections?"

"Go away! I'm here at a party!" Frank snapped back as we rushed into the Jockey Club lobby.

To our surprise, the press was not confined to a specific area, which is unusual at a private party. Maxine continued to hound Frank, and every time Sinatra started to greet someone or stand by as he was introduced, Maxine would move in. For a while, Sinatra held his tongue, but finally Maxine made the mistake of taking hold of Barbara Marx's arm. Frank, now the aroused protector, spun around and snapped, "Drop dead, creep! Why don't you get lost!"

She replied inaudibly, standing in front of us with an empty on-the-rocks glass in her hand. Frank reached into his pocket and pulled out two dollars. Stuffing them into her glass, he said, "You've been laying down all your life, you might as well get paid for it."

But she wouldn't give up. "Frank, what does that mean?" she asked with demure persistence.

He reached over and whispered in her ear something that neither I nor anyone else but Maxine heard.

Frank, whose neck had by then turned bright red, turned angrily to Barbara and said, "Let's get the hell out of here!" With that, he stormed from the club and into his limo. Dismayed, I remained behind to assess the damage.

To Sally Quinn, who was also covering parties for the *Post,* Maxine blurted out, "He called me a cunt!" By then, the word had flashed all over the Jockey Club that a scene had occurred. I fled to the bar and had three hasty Cuttys.

When I returned home much later, Frank was still sitting up in the living room in his immaculately pressed suit, furious and glaring, while Barbara sat next to him, quiet and pale. No words were spoken for a long time. As if he were sighing, Frank finally said, "I knew we should have never gone to that party."

The next day, the *Post* ran the incident as its biggest feature piece of the evening. As angry as the moment it happened, Sinatra sent our chauffeur to the drugstore to buy two aerosol cans of Pristine, while he dashed off an angry note. He was all set to send the whole package off by messenger to Maxine's office, but Mickey Rudin saw to it that the package was never delivered, adding to me *sotto voce,* "He'll cool down."

The rumors started flying immediately as to who was going to sue whom. Frank was prepared for the worst and talked to lawyers about filing a libel suit. The *Post,* I was told, took the position that Maxine would be on her own in either initiating a suit or defending herself against Frank's. Fortunately for all concerned, tempers cooled on both sides, and no further action was taken. It had been an unpleasant incident, but after all, a trivial one. It would have been folly to make more of it.

Once the inauguration party agenda had cleared, the executive branch of the government settled into its new term. Prior to the Cheshire incident, Richard Nixon—through Bob Haldeman and then me—had invited Sinatra to entertain at the state dinner for visiting Italian Prime Minister Giulio Andreotti on April 17. Now the White House grapevine informed me at the end of January that, because of Frank's recent bad press, his White House command performance might be canned. I spoke to Agnew about it, and he was sympathetic, saying, "That would be terrible after all Frank's done for us."

"Let me handle this one, sir. They aren't going to pull this kind of crap!" By his immediate return to the paper work on his desk, I gathered that Agnew was willing to let me try!

I invited Los Angeles *Times* Washington correspondent Bob Shogun to lunch at Sans Souci and outlined exactly what was happening behind the scenes, including Nixon's change of heart. The official announcement of Sinatra's performance had not hit the press and by leaking it, I hoped that it would become diplomatically impossible for Nixon to renege on the invitation without much embarrassment.

The story appeared the following day, and shortly thereafter, the first rumors of my impending termination.

The Nixon White House had just about had it with me. All through the inauguration and afterward, I had been appearing in the social pages as a high-profile administration host who received an average of twenty-five embassy and society invitations a week. This was something Henry Kissinger could get away with, but who was I? My interfering in Nixon's dump-Sinatra maneuvering was just about the last straw as far as the Oval Office was concerned.

On February 2, much to my surprise, Louise Gore was queried by a *Washington Star* columnist about Peter Malatesta's imminent firing. Apparently, the grapevine hadn't told me everything, but Agnew did when he promptly called a one-to-one meeting in his office shortly after.

Even though my job was on the line, Agnew was considerably more glum than the occasion warranted. What I did not know was that my difficulties were the least of his concerns. That very morning, he had received some bad news about his old friend Lester Matz in Baltimore, who had just implicated Agnew in a payoff bribery scandal. The usual Agnew warmth and our rapport as pals were absent. This was not the same man with whom I had so flippantly downed Chivas on-the-rocks.

"Are you happy, Peter?" he asked. Without waiting for an answer, he went on. "I'm not going to be traveling much in 1973," he said. "The need for a senior traveling aide of your caliber isn't as pressing."

"What are you trying to tell me, sir?"

He leveled with me. It had been "strongly suggested" by the White House that Agnew remove Vic Gold and me. Agnew started to paint a picture of my job that he thought I wouldn't like. "Because we're not going to be on the road much, are you sure you won't get bored with nine-to-five office hours?" Agnew asked.

I was perplexed, as I considered myself more a part of a large-scale drive toward 1976 than an ordinary 1973 model bureaucrat. The Vice President didn't need to be as evasive with me as he was being.

He mentioned that I probably had the option of a higher paying job, through the efforts of the President's personnel office. Maybe I could even land a high-ranking slot like assistant governor-general to the Samoa Islands. Geeze, is that far enough away? I thought. After twenty minutes of his "plums," I came out with it. "Do you want me to leave?"

"No, no," Agnew answered quickly. "I want what's best for *you.*"

"Well," I said, "I'm happy staying right here. Okay?"

"Okay!"

Later that afternoon, as I sat back at home with an enormous scotch and soda, Sinatra was reassuring. "You've gotta forget that petty office stuff, Pete. There's always going to be somebody out to get you. Look at me!" I laughed it off, and once my nerves were a bit more settled Frank rattled off some of the minor irritations Agnew had with me. (For example: "Why do you sleep in the back of the limo on the way to the airport?")

Before I realized he was teasing, I explained that Agnew liked to keep to himself on those short jaunts and I found it as good a time as any for twenty winks. "If he wants to talk, Frank, he'll wake me up!" Perhaps I was overstepping my bounds, but Sinatra was sure Agnew's personal disposition toward me was on solid ground.

My reasons for wanting to stay were obvious. My social identity in Washington was just becoming established. Granted, the White House didn't like the newspaper articles about a row of limos lingering at my home until three in the morning, but the rest of the Capital seemed amused by it. I not only had a sizable investment in Agnew, I now had a personal identity as "Host Peter Malatesta." I was beginning to come into my own as a social figure and, frankly, I enjoyed it.

For the next couple of months, I didn't travel much. The Veep alternated aides on his overnighters, or Art Sohmer would assume my normal role. It was clear that I was deliberately being distanced from the Veep, but it didn't bother me. I was still busy at the office with various requests from people all over the country who were trying to get to Agnew. A western governor wanted a meeting; Rod Laver's housekeeper's visa was up; a mayor in Ohio wanted a better chunk of revenue sharing. Those breather months at my desk in Washington were a relief in some ways. But as far as the Nixon people were concerned, their back-door thrust to put my social activities on ice backfired, since being off the road gave me more time to entertain more vigorously than ever.

There was no reason not to. Henry Kissinger apart, we were the only administration figures working the candlelight circuit. Kissinger, as foreign affairs adviser, had slowly built his career as a high-profile socialite, and there wasn't much Nixon could do, or wanted to do, about that. I may not have cultivated the anonymity the Nixonians expected of a person in my lowly staff position, but as long as Agnew remained tolerant of my behavior, nobody was going to stop me from enjoying myself.

Agnew, Nixon, and Sinatra shared a common distrust of the press, and they were all, in their very different ways, suspicious of my running dialogues with gossip columnists. But I saw reporters as allies, and as long as I didn't verbally step on one of the boss' toes, I felt I was safe in my own ball park.

I learned to screen my invitations ruthlessly. I would respond most enthusiastically to the larger, more social embassies, such as France, Greece, Iran, Morocco, Saudi Arabia, Jordan, or Tunisia. At the same time, I tried to be quick to entertain as many of the local socialites I had been meeting as possible. These black-tie-ers, often seen as the backdrop crowd at parties, were the bread and butter of Washington, and since I was growing to love the city, it was time for me to cultivate more than just visiting celebrities, ambassadors, and Republican biggies. If I were truly going to be an independent social entity, mixing and mingling with these people was a must.

Of course, I wasn't the only greenhorn trying to find a place in the Washington social hierarchy. I was fascinated by the rising career of 28-year-old, P.R. attorney Steve Martindale. Dubbed "The Kid from Pocatello" by the press, this newcomer was pinned with a reputation for inviting VIP "A" to a dinner party and then asking VIP "B" to attend, on the basis of "A" being there. Seemingly playing both ends against the middle, he was gradually building a strong guest list of regulars, although many of the powerful in attendance admitted, in the early days, of not knowing anything about their enigmatic host.

He seemed to be on top of the world. Kissinger, John Lennon and Yoko Ono, Art Buchwald, Martha Graham, Daniel Ellsberg, Mary Martin, and Anita Loos were all seen being wined and dined by the kid from Pocatello. But one Sunday morning, as Martindale read his copy of *The Washington Post,* he knew it was not going to be one of his better days.

Sally Quinn, a writer noted for spunky and controversial pieces, published an inordinately long article that could have spelled doomsday for the handsome, young social adventurer. She outlined his alleged "A-will-get-you-B" methods and implicitly accused him of ruthless and doggedly persistent social climbing. Many years later, Steve confided to me that it was like "having group therapy in front of a million people." Even Gary Trudeau, in his high-spirited "Doonesbury" cartoon strip, took a teasing shot at Martindale's social aspirations.

But Martindale's activities were far from being short-circuited. What Sally Quinn failed to notice was the fact that Steve Martindale was basically a likable and bright host. Even though many guests, including myself, sometimes wondered why they were invited, they always left his dinner parties with a good feeling about him. His success was finally determined by his personality, and no single newspaper article, no matter how long or scathing, was going to break it. And that is why Martindale, a clever and solicitous host, still entertains with frequency and pizzazz.

Others who also were not in obviously powerful positions won success in different ways. One popular hostess, Ina Ginsburg, became a kingpin within her own arts-oriented groups and gradually became a top hostess. After her separation from her high-powered attorney husband, David Ginsburg, Ina could have faded quickly into obscurity. But she held on, joined various charitable committees, and developed lively friendships with the diverse likes of Andy Warhol, Joan Kennedy, Henry and Muffie Brandon, Chuck Percy, and Claiborne Pell. Soon, her parties became noted for their unusual mix of people who could hardly expect to be brought together in any other setting. That Ina eventually became one of Washington's favorite hostesses says a lot for daring and imagination.

A few folks in town were cultivating their social prowess with a more basic and less cunning facilitater—money. For the pleasantly phlegmatic retired furrier Sidney Zlotnick and his wife, Evelyn, twenty-five years of hosting two to three sit-down dinners a week for twelve to forty people may have been laborious (and perhaps unexciting) but it eventually resulted in their being regarded as a kind of social fixture.

Another couple, the Mandy Ourismans, were very popular when I first arrived. The Ourismans were the well-polished and tanned epitome of the country-club set. Mandy was affectionately nicknamed "Mr. Clean," and Betty Lou exuded all the right social graces. They parleyed wholesome activities like good golf games and mid-afternoon poolsiders into a top social berth. Politically powerful? No, but they certainly hosted enough memorable buffets and lavish Christmas parties to give the impression that they ran the city.

The most vivid example that I found of a socialite who combined professional livelihood with entertaining was the Viscountess Gertrude D'Amecourt, the woman who located the house for Sinatra and me. People were unsure what actually happened to the viscount, but be she divorced, widowed, or separated, Gertrude bore her title well in a title-hungry town. Other socialites often delighted in introducing the elegant viscountess to their out-of-town friends, and Gertie always got more than her share of invites.

D'Amecourt's own parties were usually eight-to-ten, black-tie, sit-down affairs and she particularly liked to work the western European countries. I could always count on seeing the ambassadors of Austria, West Germany, Switzerland, France, and such at Gertie's table, and she was gracious enough to make sure I got to know them all.

These gatherings did far more than just feed foreigners. D'Amecourt had a thriving Embassy Row real estate office and the contacts and leads she developed over candlelight kept her sales staff jumping. There was never any doubt as to what she was up to, but no one minded and her company's track-record speaks for itself.

Allison La Land's motives were less clear-cut. Here was a socialite who was apparently not affiliated with either the Republicans or the Democrats, but who seemed anxious to court whomever was in power. Washington's top-hatters could understand socialites who kept their hole cards face-down on the table—be they aggressive attornies, chic realtors, patronesses of the arts, or wealthy retirees—but Allison La Land had no visible motives, no apparent source for her wealth, and her personality, though far from unpleasant, was not really gregarious.

She quickly included me on her guestlists, but only she knew why. Yet Allison hosted memorable parties. Her "bag" was the senatorial and ambassadorial arena, and she drew big names effortlessly.

Perle Mesta once quipped that in D.C., all a hostess needed to do to draw a crowd was hang a pork chop in the window. Allison's elegant entertainments offered a good deal more than pork chops, but I could never fully understand why she bothered. During the Nixon administration, she made a point of entertaining powerful Republicans. With the advent of the Carters, she immediately joined the Women's National Democratic Club and began entertaining powerful Democrats. No sooner had the Reagans taken over the Oval Office than she began letting it be known that "Some of my best friends are Republicans."

Many others made a combination-platter out of the above people's acts and served it up any way they could. For my part, I decided to take a lesson from my roommate and do it "My Way."

Two blocks up the street from our house stood the Gothic and imposing French Embassy. I had been invited to a typical stand-up six-to-eight cocktail party and chose this occasion to make my first independent social move—that is, without FAS as co-pilot. I called the best caterer and made arrangements for an elegant nine o'clock supper for thirty to forty people. Without one single invited guest, I hired a pianist, four additional uniformed servants, and decorated the house with a lavish arrangement of candles and flowers. A nice setting, but no players yet!

I went to the French Embassy that evening with one thing in mind—to pick off those black-tie-ers on the social circuit I wanted to get to know on my own. I walked up to prominent people I had seen at parties for over a year, stuck out my hand, smiled and reintroduced myself. My usual line that night was, "I live just down the street and I'd love for you to come by around nine for a little supper." The responses, as I moved through the party, were enthusiastic. I was convinced once and for all that the social lions whose names dominated the gossip columns were entirely available.

What worked for me more than anything that night was the impact my guests felt walking into what appeared to be a catch-as-catch-can gathering and seeing everything needed for a smashing party. I had to bet a walloping catering bill on it—and it worked!

Frank was still suffering from the aftermath of the Cheshire affair. He felt that his reputation had been tarnished and his phobia about adverse press attention had grown out of all proportion. Still there was something to be said for the "jaded" attitude of the working press toward Frank. He could definitely be cantankerous and most often it was that side of him that caught many a reporter's eye.

After talking it over, we decided that a party format was the best means of clearing the air. Why not have Frank host a bash exclusively for prominent journalists? Naturally, we would add a few local socialites to round out the scene, but this party, while being a lively soirée, would be the first time Frank opened our doors to the "enemy camp."

The guest list was encouraging. *Newsweek*'s Mel Elfin, NBC's Nancy Dickerson, columnist Victor Lasky, Jim Wooten of *The New York Times,* ABC's Herbert Kaplow, syndicated columnist Jack Anderson, the L.A. *Times'* Bob Shogun, *Time* magazine's Bonnie Angelo, Hearst's Marianne Means, among others, accepted. Although several had met Frank before, most hadn't. It promised to be a challenging evening.

Sinatra met the challenge beautifully. Frank was as warm and gracious as a newly appointed diplomat, with plenty of gentle, intelligent things to say, accented by an unusually low-keyed demeanor. In short, Francis Albert was a perfect gentleman.

This astonished some of our guests. The "bad boy" image he had been tagged with by the press seemed awkwardly inaccurate for this quiet man with sparkling blue eyes who chatted knowledgeably about fine wines and great art. Had the cameras been rolling, Sinatra would have nailed down his second Oscar.

On the heels of our press petting, I tossed the first of several parties for Eva Gabor. She and Sinatra, during a period when they were both single, had a friendly liaison. It didn't end in marriage, as we know, but it did result in a continuing friendship that, to my knowledge, they still enjoy.

When Eva started visiting us in Washington, she was dating a businessman named Frank Jameson, whom she later married. Jameson is a huge, overpowering kind of guy, but pleasant and easygoing when you get to know him. At first, I thought him a bit overbearing, but then I quickly concluded that someone of my modest stature is bound to feel overborne by anyone who's six-foot-five.

Eva and Frank were often guests at the house. I would move out of the master bedroom and put Eva into my room, because she loved it. It had a huge bathroom with a sunken marble tub, a sitting room with a fireplace, a walk-in wardrobe, even a trapeze over the bed—a real Gabor setup. I would put Frank Jameson in what we called the Blue Room, which was also Sinatra's bedroom when Frank was in town.

They always behaved with perfect propriety, but for fun I'd take bed checks at night via the intercom. I'd say, "This is the chaperone here! I just wanted to check and make sure you were both in your own rooms. During this courtship, I don't want any hanky-panky going on. I don't run that kind of house!" Sophomoric as all this was, they both seemed to find it hilarious.

Eva, with her "Peter dahling," and I always enjoyed "operating" in Washington. A short time after her first party, I was at my office in the White House and a very proper, competent, and fine lady by the name of Ruth McCawley, my secretary, answered the phone. It was morning and Eva's voice on the phone was unmistakable.

"Dahling, this is Eva Gabor. Vere's my little Peter?"

Ruth wasn't used to that kind of dialogue over the White House phones. Most calls there are a little more official than that. But my Hollywood friends tickled her.

"Mr. Malatesta is in with the Vice President. Do you want me to disturb him?" Ruth was, as always, official.

"Don't disturb him, dahling. Just have him call me when he gets out of the meeting."

And Ruth, not knowing that Eva was a guest at the house, said, "Well, Miss Gabor, where shall he call you?"

"Vy, dahling, tell him to call me at home, of course. I'm in his bed as usual . . ." With that, Eva hung up.

I came back from the Vice President's office. Ruth was shuffling papers with more intensity than I have ever seen and her face was half-red.

I asked, "Are there any messages?"

"Yes," she said. "Mr. Stevenson called about lunch and a meeting with Mr. Carpenter and, uh, Miss Gabor called."

"Oh, she did." By this time, I had a little smile on my face. "Did she leave a message?"

Ruth replied, as fast as anybody could, "Shejustsaidtotellyou-shesathome . . . and . . . she's in *your* bed!" And with that, she rushed out of the office and I howled. It took me the better part of an hour to persuade her that things aren't always as they appear.

The Gabor sisters, as we all know, have a great collection of baubles. Eva has a gang of rubies that are incredible: There is a necklace, a ring, and matching earrings—worth a ton. One night, after we had returned from an embassy reception, I said, "Eva, although the house is secured as far as the locks on the doors and windows, you wore a lot of jewelry tonight and I'm concerned. I don't have a safe here."

She replied, "Dahling, don't fret. Ve girls know what to do with our jewelry."

The next morning, I went down to the kitchen. I had fixed some marinara sauce the night before and let it mature on the stove overnight. When I got up, I felt like having scrambled eggs and a steak with a little red sauce on top. I fired up the sauce and, after thirty or forty seconds, took the wooden spoon out to stir it and I heard the damnedest clunk.

I thought, What in God's name is in my sauce?

Only about six hundred thousand dollars' worth of rubies. I shook my head. Who else would have thought of putting red rubies in a red tomato sauce on the back burner? What jewel thief would have possibly gone through the marinara sauce?

I thought, Well, I'll get even with this little fox. I took the jewels out of the sauce and turned up the flame. The aroma of the simmering marinara didn't take long to permeate the house. In fifteen minutes or so, Eva came flying down the stairs in her long chiffon, saying, "My God, vhat are you cooking in the kitchen vit my rubies?" I had to stop her before she plunked her hands into the hot tomatoes.

Sometimes when Frank Jameson was off on a business trip, I would act as Eva's escort at various social functions. One particular night, we had a few drinks at a party. Eva hardly drinks—and then only champagne—but two or three glasses of the bubbles and she's got a great buzz, and the next day it's always, "Dahling, I have a terrible overhang."

After this particular cocktail party, we were heading over to Georgetown for dinner. We were driving down P Street when we came to a stunning yellow Federalist house just before you reach the corner of Wisconsin and P. We were in traffic in the limousine, waiting for the light to change in front of this beautiful place. Eva said, "Dahling, that's such a lovely home. Vy don't we buy it?"

I said, "Well, that sounds reasonable to me."

We jumped out of the limo, which was still in traffic, and rang the doorbell. It was eight o'clock at night. A most proper black butler came to the door. He politely but casually recognized my friend even before I had a chance to make our introductions.

"We would like to know who owns the house," I asked. "Miss Gabor thinks she would like to buy it."

Suavely ignoring the fact that we were plainly a little tipsy, this highly formal butler announced that the house belonged to a Mrs. Firestone (as in radials) and graciously showed us the downstairs. He said that, to his knowledge, the house was not for sale. He asked for our address and phone number. If Mrs. Firestone, who was not at home, had any interest in selling the property, she would reply accordingly.

A month later I got a marvelously gracious note from Mrs. Firestone herself. She said she was flattered that Eva and I had dropped by and was pleased that we liked her home. It wasn't for sale, she said, but she hoped we'd call again, at which time she'd try to make arrangements for us to see some of the upstairs rooms.

So much for the house on P Street.

Contrary to the image Eva portrayed on her television series as a dizzy blonde dummy, she has a great business head. I don't know how much formal education she has, but she goes through what I call ED&L (Eva Deduction and Logic), and she always comes up with the right answers—although the logic by which she gets there would stagger you. For that matter, Frank Jameson's hunches aren't to be sneezed at, either.

Some time after our real estate excursion, Frank Jameson and Eva invited Rockwell International President Bob Anderson and his delightful bride-to-be, Diane, to be their guests for some of my home cooking. Anderson and Jameson shared mutual business interests and were close personal friends to boot. Anderson is another one of those guys with a rough and tough exterior but inside is as nice as they come.

After a few drinks, the two of them took to teasing another dinner guest, stockbroker Bill Cook, about being able to deliver tips on the stock market. Cookie began to get defensive and finally, under pressure, curtly informed them that they should "short" soybeans on the commodities market. "Short soybeans!" Frank laughed. "Imagine that! Short soybeans! I can hardly say it!"

But Cook had sounded impressively certain and, after a few more drinks, Jameson marched upstairs and returned with his checkbook. "Bill, I'm making this out for ten thousand. I'll try those soybeans." Anderson watched with amused amazement and told Bill he'd also be hearing from him soon. Oh boy, I thought. Soybeans are about to become the latest craze on Embassy Row! Cook, utterly flabbergasted but still very serious, took the ten thousand in new business and scurried home.

When Bill called the next morning, he was a good deal soberer and clearly apprehensive: "I was only kidding last night, Peter. I'm not really sure about those goddamn soybeans!"

"Ah, go for it, Bill," I replied, laughing off his worry. "It's only money."

As fate would have it, the soybean market began to plunge a few days later. The investment Jameson made was, in effect, betting that it would. Within a couple of weeks, Bill Cook's dinner-table outburst had made Jameson a very tidy sum of money.

Not to be outdone by her beau, Eva got on the phone to Bill Cook a short time later.

"Bill, my dahling, I just met the most lovely man in the world at a dinner party last night."

"Oh really?" Bill sighed.

"He's so marvelous," Eva continued. "His name is John Kluge and his company is Metromedia. Do you know it? Such a nice man! I want to buy some of that divine stock, okay dahling?!"

Bill Cook, an astute and conservative stockbroker, was dismayed by Eva's rationale. "You shouldn't buy stock just because somebody is nice!"

"Never mind," she retorted. "I vant to buy Metromedia at ten dollars a share; it's a bargain! And he vas such a dahling man, I can't tell you how much I enjoyed him."

Incorrigible! Bill thought, as he arranged the purchase. But of course Metromedia skyrocketed to 107, Eva flipped her wig, and Bill Cook took another good, hard look at ED&L.

Eva was also no dummy when it came to enjoying herself on the party circuit. She and Jameson had come to know a variety of Washingtonians and naturally my guest lists revolved around that fact. A movie star visiting the Capital isn't nearly as interested in meeting other stars as in tipping a few with the "in" powers. At Eva's first party, we entertained senators Goldwater and Tower, the ambassadors of Austria, Argentina, and Spain, Nixon's own Rosemary Woods, a coterie of miscellaneous admirals, generals, and enough socialites to keep the deck from looking too stacked.

Two days after Eva's first party, I had the opportunity to fete Rosalind Russell and her husband, Freddie Brisson. The usual clique of White Housers attended, and the Brissons brought out no less than five ambassadors, the most interesting to me being the then-ambassador from Iran, Ardeshir Zahedi, if only because this shy man was on the verge of becoming one of the most popular, lavish hosts the Capital has ever seen. His generous and expensive hospitality was soon to become legendary, but at this time he was content to sit on enormous, overstuffed pillows on the floor and, when the wee small hours crept along, to kick off his shoes. Quietly listening to the music, he seemed to be a passive guest until he'd suddenly perk up and introduce the remaining guests to Persian parlor games. A hundred and one different variations, but every one ending up with a chance to kiss a pretty girl, with an extra peck or two for our lovely guest of honor, Roz.

Roz Russell had many assets as a guest, not the least of them being her good-humored accessibility. Many guests of honor remain aloof and cautious, but Roz was a textbook example of one who wasn't. Laughing, joking, and whispering secrets to people she had never met before, Roz was unequalled in her warmth and charm. Even more amazing, though at the time I was unaware of it, was that all the while she was in great pain. She was close to death at the time of our party, but she was the most alive person in the room.

One fringe benefit of living with Sinatra was the use of the black Fleetwood Cadillac sedan he had brought down from New York. It was pointless to leave it sitting in our circular driveway for days on end, so I began riding it to work. Inevitably, this produced another typical Washington flap. It was understood that presidential aides were given staff cars, usually a modest Chrysler, and the rest of the aides drew from a small carpool for official business only. Now here I was arriving daily in a chauffeured Fleetwood, and in the fraternity of the White House everybody notices everything, even the President.

That became acutely apparent the night Sinatra finally performed at the White House for Prime Minister Andreotti of Italy. Surprisingly, I had been invited to the reception, even though I hadn't been wholly forgiven for spilling the beans about the near-cancellation of Frank's appearance months before.

Richard Nixon, at least in public, showed a marginal friendliness for me because I had worked as his aide in 1961, and perhaps because I was related to the Hopes. In the past, as I went down the White House receiving lines during his administration, I would always be greeted with the same "How are Bob and Dolores?" After perhaps a half-dozen receptions, however, Pat Nixon started noticing the pattern and, during the Italian reception, said to her husband, "Can't you ever ask him anything besides that?"

So the President asked me, "How is Mr. Agnew?"

I said, "Marvelous. How's your family?"

To that, Nixon replied, "I hear you've got a new car."

"Oh, it's not that new, sir. It's a couple of years old."

Two days later, my driver was told that he could no longer wait for me inside the West Executive parking lot. When I asked about the sudden change in privileges and the unusual aspects of the directive, I was told the order came out of Mr. Haldeman's office.

I was attending a small dinner party at the cliffside home of the late Jack Kauffmann, then a co-owner of *The Washington Star.* Without thinking, my date for the evening blurted out when surveying the crowd, "I've got to remember which one I'm with tonight." While not spoken as an insult, it did remind me that a small number of single people on the candlelight circuit attended a very large number of parties. And that gave me an idea. Why not host my kind of party exclusively for bored singles? As simple as it sounds, it was an almost unheard-of concept in Washington.

Along with stockbroker Bill Cook and Mississippi congressman Dave Bowen, I decided to round up all the old, familiar singles, add some new ones, and throw the cat in a bag. As the plans for the buffet supper got under way, Nixon's assistant chief of protocol, Nick Ruwe, joined in, and my friend Virginia Page suggested still another bachelor who might add to the evening: the prosperous, young Tongsun Park.

The rules on the invitation were elementary: Anyone attending with an escort would not be admitted. Among those who heeded the call to arms were NBC's Douglas Kiker, congressmen Sonny Montgomery and John Brademas, author Allen Drury, and perky Ann Howard, Hubert Humphrey's niece. Tongue-in-cheek all the way, millionaire Jack Kauffmann and his wife, Patsy, chaperoned the affair.

While no one was pushed in the pool and all the ladies left with their honor intact, the party did showcase Park, who had been on the periphery of Washington's social columns until then. At the time, he was all too visible on the front page of the society section, playing the piano. It was soon after that the boyish, chubby-cheeked Korean met Tandy Dickinson, a sultry divorcée with a lion's mane of blonde hair. From the humble beginnings of a simple bachelor's bash, Washington's social life was to be rocked with excitement and confusion by this pair a few years later. Among the other fruits of that party was an eventual business liaison between Park and myself that would see the first truly swank private nightclub in Washington. Park, like Agnew, was headed for the history books.

Neither Sinatra nor I was interested in entertaining on strictly a partisan level. We often joked that some of our best friends were Democrats who happen to be holding their 1974 congressional kick-off dinner in late May. At the time, Washington seemed to roll up the sidewalks after 11:00 P.M., so I could understand why the social press found it strange and even absurd that I would host a late supper party that didn't begin until midnight. The simplest explanation was that there was no other place to go, period. Even the gas stations were closed. And besides, who could resist a midnight supper with Milton Berle?

Uncle Miltie had been keynote speaker at the Democratic gala earlier in the evening and, perhaps, to some guests at my party who had attended the fund raiser, it seemed like a rerun when Berle went into his schtick about the GOP. "You can recognize a Republican by the company he keeps and the companies who keep him. . . . Nixon left today on a trip to visit all our friendly allies. . . . He'll be back tomorrow."

Word had leaked out in the columns that I was receiving some important Democrats after their gala, and during Berle's keynoter, a heckler came on stage, shouting some foolishness about the comedian being a hypocrite. Later, Berle "baptized" me in scotch for getting him into trouble during his monologue. "You Republicans really *bug* me, Peter."

Turning his wit on a laughing Hubert Humphrey, he chided, "It's tough to be a public figure, Hubert! One week on the cover of *Time,* the next week doing it!" Watergate was then becoming a primary target on the joke-rounds, and Berle's jesting to HHH was actually prophetic, albeit on the other side of the fence.

While slightly to the right of "Babylon," the 24th Street house was getting to be fertile ground for a scandal, if only by implication.

"What were all those big shots really doing there, up at all hours?" "Is it all one big party after another?" "How do they get any work done?" Those whispers bothered the White House more than they concerned me, but an opportunity arose to serve up our serious side. The day after the Berle bash, I loaned the house to my good friend and neighbor Bess Abell, who arranged a private luncheon for the house's former owner, Arthur Krock, the distinguished retired bureau chief for *The New York Times.*

Krock had just published a new book, *Myself, When Young,* and it featured a photograph of the house on its cover. In Washington, that can be reason enough to host an afternoon get-together. Krock told me that every President since Herbert Hoover had visited the house, and he wanted to know if and when Richard Nixon would be coming over. I nervously hid a big smile and explained very formally that Vice President Agnew had paid several calls to the dwelling but President Nixon had not yet done us the honor.

The cast Krock drew for his lunch was nothing if not impressive. My mind boggled as Chief Justice Earl Warren of the Supreme Court arrived, followed by Justice William O. Douglas, former Kentucky governor Earle Clements, *The New York Times'* Scotty Reston, TV's John Charles Daly, former ambassador and senator John Sherman Cooper and Kentucky senator Marlow Cook. It was not exactly the kind of poolsider Eva or Francis Albert might put together, but it also wasn't a party any of the Nixonians were going to grumble about, and I made damn sure the columnists heard about it. It's a shame that the chain of presidential visitors to the house was broken, but somehow I felt that even Richard Nixon's presence wouldn't stop the grumbling of White House gremlins.

I had, by now, learned a great deal about the living habits and life-style of my famous roommate. Perpetually a late riser, Frank seldom was seen before 11:00 A.M. He was usually very quiet in the morning and short on dialogue, save a swift "Hi there!" Dressed in his orange bathrobe and silk pajamas, clean-shaven and perfectly groomed, he enjoyed making his own breakfast, the remains of which he would always diligently clean up. Frank was fastidious about cleaning. He methodically straightened his bedroom every morning and carefully arranged his wardrobe. It always fascinated me to see the great "Las Vegas swinger" shining his boots every day as if it were his sole profession.

I remember him as a man unable to pass an untidy bookcase or a crooked painting. Full ashtrays were a particular source of irritation, and even in sight of a servant, he was always emptying them. When sitting at a table, be it at home or at a restaurant, Frank would vigorously attack any errant crumbs on the tablecloth with the crisp edge of a matchbook flap.

Frank liked to cook. He insisted on elbow room in the kitchen and often cooked alone, but I liked to watch him from a distance because his methods are so different from mine. When I cook, the kitchen looks like a battlefield when I'm done. But Frank is a neat perfectionist. For example, he'd carefully peel a single clove of garlic with a knife and fork, making a great and time-consuming effort never to touch the clove with his hands.

One evening, rather than cook at all, Frank had a sudden and great urge: "Any good pizza in town, Peter?"

A touch chagrined, I admitted pizza was not one of D.C.'s shining glories: "They all taste like cardboard in this town, Frank!"

"Well, I feel like pizza," he said as he drifted into another room. I heard him make a few short calls and then he returned, all smiles, saying, "It's all set."

"What is?"

"The pizza. It'll be here by ten o'clock."

Frank had called Washington's National Airport, where he kept his jet on 24-hour standby, and told the pilot to "take that baby to La Guardia for a pick-up." He then called a limousine service in New York and told them to fetch the pizzas from an upper East Side joint he loved and "get them to La Guardia." He arranged for another limo to meet his jet at National and rush what was now the world's most expensive pizzas back to the 24th Street house. The entire process went as smoothly as Swiss clockwork and they arrived still warm.

They were certainly very good, but I'm still not sure whether the pizzas seemed so tasty because they were a genuine gourmet find of Sinatra's or because I was just overwhelmed by the fact that what I was eating worked out to $98.12 a slice!

I never saw Frank take a drink before the cocktail hour. He enjoyed quiet afternoons when in Washington, and, if the spirit moved him, he'd venture into a museum or gallery unescorted and often unrecognized. Art is his unabashed passion. He favored the realist school of American painting and collected the works of Guy Wiggins and Edward Hopper with a fervor. When I was with him, Sinatra was a man with few heroes in his life, but Pablo Picasso was certainly the exception. He always spoke of the man with reverence.

Moody and subject to abrupt, flashy decisions, he used to pretend to spit whenever actor Peter Lawford's name was mentioned. Bobby Kennedy was certainly no favorite either, and I always had the feeling he held RFK personally responsible for the "Mafia connection" investigations. In spite of that, Sinatra adored Jackie Kennedy Onassis—almost as much as he loved Picasso.

Whenever Barbara Marx was in town, Sinatra glowed brighter. Barbara was best labeled in those days as "a regular Joe." Beautiful, witty, and shy, she made a point of remaining loyal to her old friends even after joining Frank's world. With her feet planted firmly on the ground, she provided a sense of stability and balance for Frank. Washington also liked Barbara. Neither too reserved nor too outgoing, she had many of the same traits of manner and personality that made Princess Grace so popular. But she was still "one of the boys," who could take a joke, drink a few, and still hold her own ground. When we were together in the Springs or D.C., she neither coddled nor badgered Frank. In spite of the social whirlpool we spun in, Barbara and Frank's relationship remained a model of decorum. They never kissed and certainly never argued in public. Even today, she remains a perfect counterpoint for Frank's 1960's "Rat Pack" image.

My roommate let me in on a succinct and direct way of dealing with bothersome memorandums. Frank kept a rubber stamp at his desk, pounding out "WRONG!" whenever he felt something deserved it.

I liked this idea and thought it would make a handsome addition to the Vice President's desk. Frank sent me a box of "WRONG!s" and I gave them to Agnew, who was delighted, glorying in the fact he had "WRONG!" in four different colors. He soon had his staffers in a flurry. "Is my yellow 'WRONG!' wronger than your red 'WRONG!'?" Meanwhile, Agnew scampered through piles of paperwork with the playfulness of a kitten.

It was time to move into heavier equipment. "Frank," I asked, "how about a box of 'BULLSHIT' made-up in the same color scheme?"

I wasn't entirely sure how Agnew would react to this escalation, but he roared with approval. Soon Agnew's "BULLSHIT" was regularly hitting the office fan, but by then the rest of the staff had cheerfully accepted their new boss's latest toy.

It didn't take long for my invitation to boomerang. Agnew's staff had a continual problem convincing the punctual, clock-conscious Vice President that strict, one-hour lunches, even on matters of business, were impractically limiting. "What does he expect us to do, take Bryce Harlow to Burger King?" I moaned to Vic Gold after still another Agnew lecture on the subject. The Veep reminded me of a high-school principal as he'd wander the halls, making office-checks to see who was back from lunch on time. As press secretary, Vic Gold was particularly hampered since it was nearly impossible to do what he needed to in the space of an hour.

One day I left at noon for a lunch appointment with a spectacular congressional aide and locked horns with her, if you can believe it, over an aspect of revenue-sharing. When I returned, there was a handwritten vice-presidential note on my desk. "IT IS ALL RIGHT TO BE AT LUNCH UNTIL 2:15." Below the scribble were a bold, freshly stamped "WRONG!" and the tiny initials, "s.t.a."

"I've created a monster!" I groaned to Vic.

F.S. chose to spend July yachting with Barbara, and I seized the opportunity to take a much-needed vacation from Washington by visiting my friend and landlady, Virginia Page, at her home in Marbella, Spain. A small group of us went, including Bill Cook, now known in the social columns as "the pianist/stockbroker." In addition to being a fine soloist, Bill was often a party-accompanist at my home for Pearl Bailey, Sinatra, Vikki Carr, Dolores Hope, and anyone else who wanted to croon. Bill was also a close friend of Artur Rubenstein, whom I had met previously, through Bill, at Constitution Hall.

On this particular Sunday in Spain, Bill came up with a special surprise—he invited us to visit the grand hillside villa of the Rubensteins and be their guests for cocktails. On a beautiful, clear blue Mediterranean afternoon, we motored the winding roads up to Rubenstein's summer home in Costa del Sol.

As we approached the house, we could hear the maestro

practicing. We rested on his front steps, not wanting to knock on the door and disturb the music. It was so mesmerizing to hear this man practicing that we must have been on the steps for minutes before we were aware that he had stopped.

We entered applauding, and the charming old man, with his great rosy cheeks and a face like a newborn baby's, greeted us with a healthy smile and clear, dancing eyes. He and his delightful wife, Nela, were elegant hosts. It was obvious from the twinkle in his eyes and the stories he told with a freshman's vigor that Artur Rubenstein makes growing old seem like fun.

Before we left, he invited Cook to play, which I thought was quite an honor. It was the only time I can remember that Bill ever declined such an invitation, but who could blame him? Rubenstein then graciously offered to play a farewell piece for us and asked me what I liked. I requested "anything by Chopin." He chose an exquisite nocturne, which was perfect for the time of day, and we left in a state that can only be called euphoric.

The situation in Washington, when I returned, was in no way euphoric. Storm clouds were brewing for Agnew. No one on the staff had any information to back up the persistent rumors and I dismissed them, but with an uneasy apprehension. During the rest of July, Agnew made very few trips out of Washington, and then only to New York. He was strangely quiet, out-of-sorts, and distant. By now, the murmurs about Agnew's possible involvement in a Maryland kickback scandal had become loud whispers on the cocktail circuit.

Everyone near the Vice President had their own concept of the still-unspoken problem, but a *Wall Street Journal* article on August 7 exceeded our darkest dreads. It stated that Agnew was indeed under investigation by the Justice Department and could possibly be indicted. The allegations by the U.S. Attorney's Office in Baltimore included bribery, extortion, and tax fraud.

Sinatra and I had just left for a few days of golf in Palm Springs, but upon hearing the news, we turned around and flew back to Washington that same night, accompanied by Mickey Rudin. Though still disbelieving, we mobilized quickly. We met with Vic Gold, who was now back in the private sector, but still very loyal to Agnew and anxious to help. The 24th Street house became a think tank. For the next several days, we prepared a plan to present to the Vice President. Vic and I drafted a number of forceful, counterattack statements while

Rudin quietly slipped off to Baltimore for some private investigating of his own. Two days later, when we all met again, Rudin discreetly reported that his inquiries had produced evidence about Agnew that bore up the old adage that "where there's smoke, there's fire." Incredulously, I looked at Rudin and said, "Mickey, are you trying to tell me that he might be guilty of some of this garbage?"

A Rudin classic followed, "Peter, don't bore me with the facts."

Mickey curtly dismissed any further questions from us by unveiling his own plan of action. Even given the facts, Rudin was confident that if Agnew took a hard line and fought the charges in court "no twelve jurors would vote unanimously to convict him." He outlined a plan involving a group of the five best criminal lawyers in the country as a defense team for Agnew. Rudin reasoned that if Agnew would fight a long court battle, some of the Watergate pressure would be taken off Nixon. "After all," Mickey pointed out, "a court case like this could drag on for years and the man *is* innocent until proven guilty." With a dark cloud over Agnew, Rudin reasoned no one would dare attempt to force Nixon out of office because Agnew would automatically become President, even if he were still on trial. The possibility of impeaching Agnew by the Congress was, at best, remote, said Rubin. "All he's got to do is stay in and fight. The impeachment route is no way for him to go."

Armed with Rudin's theory and with his defense lawyers in the wings, we met with Agnew. Vic and I entered the Veep's office and told him his credibility was at stake and, "For God's sake, come out punching, sir." He agreed with us. At this point, an old-fashioned pep talk seemed to be all the medicine needed. Unknown to us, however, there was to be an entire other world of plea-bargaining sessions that Agnew was pursuing to save his own skin. In fact, I doubt that Agnew ever took Rubin's game plan seriously, although he was certainly aware of it.

I made a number of discreet calls to people whom I knew would be close to the situation. No one wanted to say anything, and everywhere there was an atmosphere of extreme caution. Finally I called White House confidant Bryce Harlow, a straight shooter who was very close to the Vice President. Harlow was my political mentor and a man I trusted, but for the first time, Bryce was evasive with me and calculated with his words; he was definitely not the same man I breakfasted with monthly. There was now no doubt in my mind that Agnew's blood was in the water and we were in a fight for survival.

I reported to Frank, Mickey, and Vic my distressing non-conversation with Harlow. Vic and I speculated on a manipulation by the President to throw Agnew to the wolves in order to take the heat off his own Watergate involvement. That would, of course, have been contrary to Rudin's scenario, but it seemed no less logical.

The miasma of the Watergate scandal had begun to infect everyone. Out of the blue one afternoon, I received a call from an investigator in Archibald Cox's office. He wanted to informally interrogate me about certain contributions made to the Committee To Re-elect the President. The donors in question were all West Coast contacts of mine. To the best of my recall, their gifts were all within the limit set by law, but Cox's office wanted to make sure, and, according to this investigator, "discuss certain other matters, in person."

I was hostile toward the call. The Washington press was filled with every leak and slip-of-the-tongue that anyone, even indirectly involved, had made. It seemed to me that the investigators were sloppy, often leaking inaccurate quotes. My hands were clean, and I knew that by demanding exactitude in the interview, they'd stay clean. Actually, the only thing I knew about Watergate was how to get to Anna Chennault's penthouse for a party.

"I'll agree, on one condition," I said to Cox's lieutenant. "The interview *must* be on a one-to-one basis. If you send two-to-one, then I'm going to want my own witness." They agreed.

Bill Rusher from the *National Review* happened to be in the office on the afternoon when the investigators arrived. After my secretary screened them and told me there were *two,* I asked Rusher to kindly wait in an anteroom. In marched a severe preppie-type in his early thirties, followed by a young sidekick.

Genuinely angry, I said, "It was made quite clear on the telephone that the interview was to be between you and me. Who's he?"

"Mr. Cox wants a witness to be present," the preppie replied.

"Fine," I said, "Then *I* want a witness to be present." With that, I called Bill Rusher in, a noted conservative journalist with whom the investigators were more than familiar. "My problem and my *only* problem with this is the way you guys twist what people tell you," I said. "If there's going to be a leak out of my office, I want a member of the press here to report it accurately."

I thought the preppie was starting to show early signs of a stroke. "We'll see about this!" he snarled. "The next time I talk to you it will be by subpoena!"

"Have it any way you want it, pal!" I shot back, with more bravado than confidence.

Arriving home that night, I laid out the day's events before Mickey Rudin.

"Let me handle this one, Peter," Mickey said reassuringly.

I listened on the extension the next morning as Rudin called my hot-blooded preppie investigator. "I represent Peter Malatesta and my client is very irritated. He's an emotional type and upset by your lack of fulfillment of commitment. He will no longer make private statements and will only address your questions if you subpoena him; in fact, he insists on being subpoenaed."

I began opening and closing my mouth, but no sounds came out. What the hell was Rudin doing?

"My client has a propensity for being rather flamboyant when he's faced with matters like this," Rubin continued, "and he wants to know well in advance when he'll be subpoenaed because he plans on alerting the press. There can be no question as to the absolute accuracy regarding his statements."

The preppie began to stutter. "He's making a mountain out of a molehill—we only wanted to talk to him for a couple of minutes!"

"Nevertheless," Mickey said flatly, "if you want to deal with my client, those are his terms."

I never heard from Cox's office again.

But to my surprise, I did hear from the FBI. A week prior to the attempted interview by the Watergate investigators, *The New York Times* printed a story alleging I had interceded with John Dean on Sinatra's behalf and had attempted to arrange quietly for an early parole for reputed Mafioso Angelo DeCarlo. The *Times* article stunned me; I had never even heard of De Carlo before I read how I tried to spring him! Equally idiotic was my alleged contact with Dean. At best, John Dean and I might just have recognized each other's faces at a cocktail party, but we never had any reason to converse about anything and hadn't.

Suing a major paper is not easy and serves to publicize the lie, so I took a cue from my roommate and let the article die its own death. As a matter of routine, the FBI called me to check out the published allegations. In a neat sworn statement, I denied every point *The New York Times* made, and the FBI pleasantly put the matter to bed.

I later found out this hearsay originated from a Capitol Hill office: another leak! Watergate Washington was virtually a sieve of misinformation; false trumpets were sounding every day. Some of it was fact, much of it fiction. What the hell, I thought. The *Times* has a Watts line; why didn't they at least call me before printing that crap! They call for every other little thing.

With my private scandals finally at bay, I returned to the Vice President's problems. Vic Gold and I decided to hold court in the Sans Souci almost every working day and lunch individually with members of the national press and anyone else in media power who would listen to us. At these sessions with *Time, Newsweek,* the *Post, The New York Times,* and Los Angeles *Times,* and such, we'd plead Agnew's case on the basis of the facts we had. We were both convinced, naively or otherwise, that Agnew's legal problems were a trumped up White House scheme. Needless to say, Agnew never bought this plan either, though it was discussed with him privately and at length.

By early September, the Vice President, weekending in Palm Springs, was in very low spirits. Now, only a small coterie surrounded him: Sinatra, Rudin, acting Chief of Staff General Mike Dunn, Doc Voss, and myself. Frank, Mike, and I decided that, come cocktail hour, we were going to have to try to turn the "old man" around. The country was expecting him to be the white knight on a big horse, and he was acting like a guilty schoolboy. Convinced of his innocence, we were becoming increasingly worried about his inertia. At the calculated time, we surrounded him, gave him his first Chivas and proceeded to lay it on him. He sat there quietly, listening to our aggressive pleas for a tougher defense. Based on the premise that he was innocent, our argument was logical, but Agnew just sipped his drink and didn't say much.

The next day, on a plane flight to Los Angeles, the Vice President asked me for a piece of paper and started to make notes. All of us were dying to peer over the "old man's" shoulder as he wrote, but no one was presumptuous enough to do so. Sinatra sat nearby, working *The New York Times* crossword puzzle and occasionally winking at me, a signal that, in everyone's mind, something was cooking with our silent friend.

We arrived at the hall and Agnew let the National Federation of Republican Women have it. They were ardent fans of his and a perfect support team for his angry words that "I have been living in purgatory. . . . I am innocent of the charges against me." The bitter rhetoric that followed clearly attacked the top Justice Department figures who had pushed for his indictment. "I will not resign if indicted!" he shouted.

As he walked off the podium, I blurted out, "That was a hell of a shot!" and I said it with all the excitement I could muster. We were going to lick this yet! Minutes later, speaking to Californian GOP leaders in private session, Agnew said his 1976 presidential aspirations were no longer realistic but that he would campaign hard for any Republican candidates who wanted his help in the upcoming congressional elections. In hindsight, that alone should have tipped me off that his rousing speech was hollow. The only way Agnew would ever give up a run at the 1976 White House was if his prosecutors had a leg to stand on. But for the time being, I kept on fighting.

Agnew's offensive posture lasted only a matter of days. Vic and I dealt off the record with the press as best we could, even though the evidence was mounting. We still accepted Agnew's explanation that the testimony being given against him in Baltimore was mere perjury, and we proceeded with righteous stamina.

The Agnew outbursts in Los Angeles had been covered on nationwide television, and the press and public alike looked forward to Agnew's next scheduled speech in Chicago five days later. The fire was fueled by Marsh Thompson, Vic Gold's low-keyed replacement as press secretary. Marsh unwittingly told the press that Agnew was "in a fighting mood." This feeling was taken for granted by the staff, but the Nixon team somehow considered the words a personal attack on the President. Thompson was promptly canned.

With the expectant press gathered at the Drake Hotel, Agnew marched to the podium and addressed the large Republican dinner with less punch than at any time in his career. "Tonight is not going to be an X-rated political show," he said. "It's just going to be PG. So if you have to go anyplace, go. A candle is only so long before it burns out."

After the speech, the press swarmed to me to unravel the

depths of the cryptic statement about a candle. Was he going to resign? Had he had it? Was this the end? Reporters for *The New York Times* and the Hearst papers immediately camped by Agnew's hotel door and waited for a further explanation. Inviting the journalists out for a drink, I did my best to brush aside the speculation.

But I couldn't refute it. None of the staff had much access to the Vice President during this time. We were compartmentalized, and no one really knew the whole story or had any significant inside information that might be useful to reporters. This, I believe, was deliberate, leaving me with little to say to the press other than "Would you like another drink?"

The next day, back in Washington, the end was in sight but, as the saying goes, we couldn't see the forest for the trees. Nothing was happening in the offices. There was a deadly stagnation in the air, as if a giant, celestial secretary had just put the whole White House on hold. Then, on October 10, at ten o'clock in the morning, notice was put out that there was to be a full staff meeting at 2 P.M. I called John Damgard in scheduling and asked him to join Vic Gold and me at the Sans Souci to try to figure out what was about to happen. With two martinis in me before noon, I got up from the table and called Mike Dunn and asked, "What's really going on?"

"I can't discuss it with you over the phone, Peter, but you'll know at two o'clock."

A slight pause, and I said, "Is it as grim as I think it is?"

"It's very grim."

With that, John, Vic, and I sat around with another drink and tried to decide what "grim" meant. At that point, we still thought "grim" meant fighting a long impeachment battle on the hill, where Agnew would be looking for Congress to be on his side.

A bit after twelve o'clock, I called Mickey Rudin in Los Angeles. "Is he going to go up on the Hill?" I asked. Big pause. "Mickey, is he going to quit? Is he going to resign?"

"I really can't say," Rudin replied. "You'll find all that out at two o'clock."

"C'mon, stop. Stop playing games with me."

Rudin's next words caught me short. "He's going to resign."

Suddenly, I felt confused and disillusioned—betrayed. Had I, after all, been nothing more than a stooge for a guilty man? I didn't know how I was going to look anyone in the face again, especially the press. "I feel like a total asshole," I told the maitre d', Paul Delisle, as I left the restaurant.

I couldn't face the two o'clock meeting. Instead, I went home and called my neighbor Bess Abell. "Bess, I need some moral support. C'mon over."

We sat in front of the television and, after the first flashing news bulletin, the phone began to ring. When Bob Shogun of the L.A. *Times* called, I launched the most vocal assault on Nixon I have ever uttered in the many years I've disliked him. It was so strong, my father called the next day from California asking, "What the hell are you thinking about?"

Two days later, the staff received word from Mike Dunn that, as part of a deal cut with the White House, every member of the Agnew staff was to be relocated in a financially compatible position. I sat in my now-defunct office, miserable and in a trance. There was a knock on my door, a door which in the past was never closed. The former Vice President walked in. "Do you mind if I sit down?" he asked.

"Of course not, sir!"

He started to thank me for the support I had given him, but still angry and depressed, I interrupted him and said, "What the hell did you do it for? If you're not guilty, why quit? How could you do it?"

Sadly, he said, "Things have happened and there are pressures that I am not at liberty to tell you about right now. I had to do what I did. Some day it will all come out. You'll have to trust me."

I dismissed his ambiguous comments as ramblings until recently, when Agnew published the suggestion that his life might have been in danger. Now it seems to me that at the time we spoke he may well have been a man with more on his mind even than impending disgrace.

But it was time to see if the pieces still fit in *my* life. I weighed very heavily the idea of returning to California, but I stopped myself. I had built a strong social life in Washington, and I would have to give up a great deal. Agnew may have had a misfortune, but there was no reason for me to leave town . . . I hoped.

While I was mulling over these worries, I received an invitation from Zahedi on behalf of the shah of Iran, announcing a party honoring His Imperial Majesty's visit to Washington. This is just what I need, I thought, a good Zahedi bash to take my mind off my troubles.

With the shah there in person, Zahedi was bound to go all out, and besides, I needed the exposure for many personal reasons—like finding a new job.

It startled me when Ardeshir called late on the day of the affair. Speaking hurriedly, he asked me if I could appear at the embassy a half-hour before the coterie of guests and press arrived. I never asked why because Zahedi hung up before I had a chance.

As requested, I arrived early, deposited my coat, and headed downstairs. Ardeshir wasted no time in hellos, grabbing me politely by the arm and rushing me into an anteroom off the main salon. "His Majesty is waiting," he said in a hushed tone. "Keep him company until the receiving line is ready; I'm running late!" With that, he opened the door and there stood the shah—alone, dressed in a trim, European-tailored black silk suit, sans the medals and heavy golden braiding which had so dazzled me in Persepolis.

At a loss for words, I ran through a computer's worth of potential conversations while Zahedi hastily re-introduced us. I worried about the subject of Agnew; would the shah bring it up? For one dizzy moment, I toyed with the idea of challenging His Highness to a game of backgammon, but though sanity prevailed, I still couldn't think of an alternative. Finally I blurted out something about the 2,500th anniversary celebration and my thrill at being able to be present. The shah seemed pleased with my enthusiasm and agreed with my comment about the unfairness of the press coverage.

To my relief, the shah then took the initiative and began talking casually about his infatuation with the city of Washington. "It's as beautiful as Paris, isn't it?" he asked, relaxing the expression on his face. "And New York? Do you enjoy New York?"

I was all set to say any number of fascinating things about how much I liked New York when, with the same gusto with which he had whisked me into this *tête-à-tête*, Zahedi threw open the doors and announced that the press and dignitaries were ready to greet His Majesty. Thus, as the Nixonian VIPs stood at attention, who should walk out with His Imperial Majesty still chatting animatedly, but Malatesta. I could see by the look on Kissinger's face that his mind was going a mile a minute trying to figure out why I was in there alone with this man. But as is typical in Washington, no one risked asking what we talked about.

For the rest of the evening, I enjoyed an unspoken but almost palpable status as the man who had a mysterious private meeting with the shah. No one but Ardeshir knew that all I had done was act as a royal babysitter, and none too competently at that. If Ardeshir had delayed his entrance another ten minutes, I could probably have dined out for a month on the strength of my mystery-man reputation.

A day or so later, I received a call from Dave Wimer, then the chief of personnel for the White House. He suggested I stop by his office. Twenty years ago, Wimer had been a night watchman at the Hope house while attending UCLA, so our ties as friends had deep roots. After kicking around a few ideas in his office, Wimer picked up the phone and called Fred Malek, then deputy director of OMB in the White House and another old pal. Wimer arranged for a meeting between himself; Malek; Tony Turner, the assistant secretary of commerce for administration; and me. "We've got the President's box at the Kennedy Center, and we can kick around something there," Wimer said.

"Great!" I laughed. Here I was, about to sit in the President's seat in the grand, red velvet Opera House, and two days before I all but called the man everything but a murderer.

During a particularly boring first act of a long-forgotten play, we went into the antique-filled anteroom behind the box and opened a bottle of champagne. Turner said, "We've created a new job at Commerce and I think it'll be good for you, and us—deputy assistant secretary for tourism."

"What's that?" I asked doubtfully.

"You'd handle Commerce's role for the Bicentennial, but you'd have to give us a couple of days to put it together."

After not too much reflection, I said, "I'll take it."

With that, we popped another bottle of champagne and went back to the presidential box. The play continued to be a bore, but the days ahead promised not to be. Now, with my working base secure, I could return to laying plans for my assault on Washington society.

Chapter Eight

In Washington, the old adage "You're only as good as you're going" is creed. Fortunately for me, party invitations, Washington's surefire social barometer, continued to arrive at my home in piles, along with dozens of notes and phone calls from my numerous friends urging me to stay.

An article that appeared in the L.A. *Times* a month after Agnew resigned, called "Former Agnew Aide Rides Out the Storm," summarized (perhaps a little too flatteringly) my position: "He is a refreshing personality in these glamourless days here. In the antisocial atmosphere of this Administration, he seems different." The article continues, quoting hostess Buffy Cafritz, "We didn't know him, but we liked him. It was the openness of the man. At parties, most Washingtonians are very busy looking around the room. The thing we noticed about Peter was that he was looking right at us!" Marlene Cimons, the writer of the piece, added kindly: "This kind of support is unique, a tribute to Malatesta from a city which characteristically excommunicates its powerless. It has not only been a source of strength for him but a major reason for his decision to stay in Washington."

Very nice, but the operative word was still "powerless." It was only a matter of two weeks after Agnew's resignation that Sinatra's secretary, Lilian Paluso, called me to make arrangements for two of Frank's more valuable paintings, a Guy Wiggins and a Maurice de Vlaminck, to be shipped back to Palm Springs, pronto. I got the picture fast. Frank has had it here, I thought.

Within days, Paluso's call was followed by one from Mickey

Rudin, confirming that Frank wanted out. Rudin said that Sinatra no longer had any use for the place and suggested I dismantle the lease that held us there. Sinatra would be "in" for one more month, in name only, and that would be the end of that.

Virginia Page was sympathetic, but she had her own plans to sell the house as soon as possible. In the interim, Eva Gabor and Frank Jameson, who had enjoyed 24th Street so much, offered to pick up Sinatra's end until the house was sold. Jameson said he had reasons to be in D.C. often, and Eva adored the Embassy Row scene. I gratefully accepted their offer.

I was truly disappointed in Frank's abrupt decision to cancel Washington. Where Sinatra and I had once averaged five phone exchanges a week when he was out of Washington, I now found we barely spoke at all after Agnew's plea of *nolo contendere.* I began to realize that my friendship with Sinatra had been more professional and less personal than I had supposed. A little depressed, I turned my thoughts to other matters.

I had been kicking around an idea for years. From the success of my parties, it was clear to me that social Washington all too often had no place to go after a typical six-to-eight cocktail party. Guests were dressed and off to a flying start by the time most affairs were ending. In many cases, there was an entire half-an-evening yet to be filled. Damn it, I thought, this city *really* needs a private club—a place to rendezvous after the first act—a place where people can see and be seen—a night spot for gossip and champagne. Maybe I could find a way to reproduce on a wider, commercial scale the ambiance and purpose of the parties I had had at my home.

Promoter C. Wyatt Dickerson, husband of former NBC newscaster Nancy Dickerson, and an attorney friend of his met with me over lunch. We hashed over my idea for establishing a private club. The city was overloaded already with formal, private, paneled haunts, but none that filled the late evening "dance and gossip" void.

Long-standing clubs in Washington had actually evolved into institutions and were, for the most part, bastions of elitism. The Metropolitan Club, for men only, was a classic case. Located near the White House, its membership was extremely exclusive, and, more to the point, it seldom offered very much to do after dinner except sniff a little cognac in the reading room by the fire. Its counterpoint for women, The Sulgrave, was a matronly version of the same Old

Washington clique. The Cosmos Club catered to scientific and political eggheads, some of whom lived (and died) there. The Alibi was another small club in the vicinity of 1600 Pennsylvania. It was the hardest of all to join, boasting a mere forty male members. The Federal City Club in Georgetown was slightly more social and had a good chef, but its activities were all over by 11:00 P.M. Tongsun Park's George Town Club was a hang-out for lobbyists and separated itself from the masses by being very expensive. The "in" country club was Chevy Chase, but it didn't think much of blacks, Jews, the nouveau-riche, out-of-towners, foreigners, well-to-do-bachelors, up-and-coming young couples, and so on. C.C.C.C. was a great place for a round of golf but an even better one for old people to take their parents to dine. The Washington Club on Dupont Circle had such a low-activity profile that even members of other clubs had no idea what went on there. On the whole, it didn't take much imagination to concede that my idea for a private nightclub was hardly vulnerable on account of stiff competition.

Dickerson thought the idea was good and his friend, a pro at putting restaurant deals together, agreed. Realization of the idea was still two years down the road, but the seed had been planted.

During the first few months after Agnew's departure, his former staff chose to remain close to each other, and we socialized as often as possible. We didn't waste time on Monday-morning quarterbacking; instead, we concentrated on making our plans for the future. Of all of us, Mary Ellen Warner, Agnew's personal secretary, and John Damgard remained the longest with the "old man," moving with him into the former Vice President's transition offices. In the face of all we had been through, it was almost ironic that the party I hosted for Sinatra's big television comeback was a glowing success.

With several TV sets placed around the double living rooms, stacks of Sinatra's new album there for the taking, and the city's top social reporters in good form, it was the best-kept secret in town that the singer and I were not only no longer roommates, but were hardly speaking. As the old Agnew gang gathered around in a family-like gesture of solidarity, I realized this party, more than any other, was pure face-saving showbiz. Not a word was whispered, but a lot of people there *needed* that party to look good, and none more than I.

Even the last great social dowager of Washington, the late

Virginia Bacon, attended and was actually surprised at what a good time she was having. "Peter, why haven't you invited me before?" she asked with unusual modesty as she sipped her second martini.

I wanted to say, "Because I've been saving you for my moment of need. I'm stacking the deck and you're my ace—Madam Credibility!" but I didn't.

As a special bonus to the evening, I hired a jazz harpist to play during cocktails and dinner, and he was an instant hit. Henry Kissinger pulled me aside and prodded me about the young man. "I've seen him before, Peter, but I don't know vere. Vat's his name?"

"Shhh." I laughed. "Don't blow the kid's cover. He's the harpist for the White House Marine Corps Band, and he's moonlighting. He could get into trouble if you say anything, Henry!"

Ten days later, when I attended a State Department reception given by "the K," I heard those same wistful strains of music and, to my not-very-great surprise, I found Kissinger was showing off his marvelous new "discovery."

Our TV party was soon followed by another Zahedi extravaganza. Liza Minnelli was appearing at the Kennedy Center, and the Iranian was going to entertain her in a manner befitting Catherine the Great. Ardeshir Zahedi was now beginning to emerge as the black-tie volcano of Massachusetts Avenue. Certainly he spared no expense in his entertainment, but I couldn't help noting that his success was due in part to that formula in which I so strongly believed: the extra glamor involved in dusting his affairs with celebrities.

Zahedi was well-connected in Washington and getting to know both Hollywood and New York—star by star—better. He understood what could be accomplished with the addition of an Oscar-winner to his guest list, and he built his glittery reputation for elegant three-ring circuses by making sure the Liza Minnellis and Liz Taylors of the world were at his parties. I'd like to think he took some of his cues from the activities of the 24th Street house, but I'd never want to detract from Zahedi's own talents as a warm, conscientious host. He was truly a natural for lavish entertaining and was very well liked. In fact, he was the best!

Each new Zahedi party outdid the previous one. Soon, the scale of his events had become spectacular. Anyone who has ventured into an expensive French restaurant has an idea what a bottle of Dom Perignon and a single spoonful of Beluga caviar cost. Try ordering unlimited quantities of both for two hundred people, throw in dozens of stuffed pheasants, Middle Eastern delicacies of every kind, a handsome orchestra, and much more and you begin to get the idea of what entertaining meant to Ardeshir Zahedi. He confided to me that in 1973 a single party's flower bill alone ran him over $5,000. And Ardeshir was good for three of those a month, interspersed with smaller, but equally well-appointed, dinners for twenty to fifty about four times a week! It somehow humbled my marinara sauce, served California-style.

The Iranian courted everyone and repeatedly was credited by prominent Washingtonians for accomplishing more P.R. for the shah than a string of Madison Avenue agencies. It was party politics at its best! While sterling silver ice-cream scoopers were used to serve up the caviar, what really brought out the guests was the simple fact that power draws power. Not to be included on Zahedi's guest list was tantamount to social exile. He overshadowed even the White House's entertaining and continually commanded at his table the likes of the Rockefellers, Hopes, Fords, Kissingers, and Humphreys. Nothing short of a revolution was going to stop his momentum.

Only once, when Barbra Streisand shyly appeared at the entrance of his great mosaic ballroom, did a Zahedi affair momentarily grind to a halt. Who could continue gobbling tiny fish eggs when the decade's most elusive superstar decides to drop by for a drink or two, shah-style? Zahedi's scene was enough to make one frequent guest, Elizabeth Taylor, drop her emeralds, which she did while dancing there a few years later.

It was Christmas 1973 and the following New Year's that saw the last of my intimate relationship with Francis Albert Sinatra. For three years, it had been a tradition to spend the holidays at Frank's and, even though he had severed his 24th Street ties, the compound in Palm Springs expected my arrival this yuletide. Frank maintained a merry holiday attitude throughout, but our personal rapport was no longer the same. The parties and guests were festive enough, but I sensed a distance between us that I was never able to put my finger on.

Through mutual friends, I was told that before my Christmas arrival Agnew had complained to Frank that I had deserted him after the resignation. I had "let Agnew down in his hour of need," I was told. Granted, I had wasted no time in finding a new job and had not waited around for Agnew eventually to hand me another position, but I had parted with Agnew as a close friend and had assured him and his staff that I was only a phone call away, should they need me for anything.

Where was Spiro coming from? Only a week before he had called me and asked me to feel out several Arab ambassadors to find out whether they'd accept an invitation to his home. He was going to throw a party for the sake of stirring up his entrepreneurial contacts with them, and once again I was to do the bird-dogging. Of those close to him, I was still the only one socially well-connected with the Arabs, with whom Agnew wanted to do business. Any use of official channels was out of the question, and I had happily agreed to feel them out prior to their receiving a formal invitation.

I had phoned Zahedi, Salah of Jordan, Senoussi of Morocco, and Al-Sowayel of Saudi Arabia for starters. The ripples of their acceptances had brought out many others. The consensus among them was a respect for the former Vice President and a generally philosophic downplay of his resignation as an American tempest in a teapot. Most ambassadors didn't claim even to understand the Watergate syndrome and still viewed Agnew as a powerful man. They would be glad to attend.

Why, then, did Agnew now choose to complain about my desertion to Frank? I still don't know, but Christmas 1973 at the compound seemed to me a graceful yacht on a stormy sea.

Back at the Commerce Department after the New Year of 1974, I shifted into full gear as deputy assistant secretary for Bicentennial affairs—shaking hands with dignitaries, ceremoniously inspecting new Amtrak trains, and generally handing out a lot of preview "Spirit of '76" tie tacks.

If there was one memorable moment during my tenure with Commerce, it occurred in East Glacier Park, Montana. Representing the U.S. Travel Service, I was invited to attend a three-day conference regarding the tourist industry and I was delighted to go. This particular jaunt came with a personal aide, first-class accommodations on Amtrak, and included a weekend in San Francisco for a stopover speech at still another conference.

I was briefed by the Department of Interior before I left on the mood and mores of the Black Foot reservation locals. There was nothing to worry about, I was told, but since the young Indians there could be hostile toward any fat cats from Washington, I was to play it cool and stick to business. I filed that in the back slat of my memory and packed my bags.

The tourist facilities at the park, within the Black Foot reservation, were operated by college kids who had lucked out on a plum summer job. After a day of meetings and agenda-tackling, I was impressed by the easygoing attitude of these perky youngsters who, in effect, ran the place.

My inveterate fascination with night life popped up again and I was dying to find out what this lively and attractive crowd did after sunset, and where. Downtown East Glacier Park, all one-half block of it, was about a quarter-mile from the lodge where I was staying. It consisted of a little general store, with an attached beer and wine cantina complete with a jukebox full of last year's hits. The guys and gals from the park staff would rally there, have a few beers, and dance the night away.

As soon as I had a chance, I hotfooted it over there, enjoying the crisp, crystal clear evening air and array of bright stars above me. They were huge that night, but not as huge as they were going to get shortly.

The kids were terrific, and I think they got a kick out of partying with the "biggie" from Washington as much as I liked dancing and joking with them. Apparently, the youngsters were surprised that this old bureaucrat even knew the words to the songs we were dancing to. A half-dozen glasses of wine later, I was ready to call it a night and truck back to the lodge.

Stepping out the door, I was suddenly faced with six or seven dark, heavy-looking cats with long, braided hair and plaid lumberman jackets: unmistakably real live Indians! My short briefing suddenly took a quick front seat and I flashed them the biggest smile I could muster.

"Hi, fellas! Nice out tonight, isn't it?"

A burly and not very attractive guy, still a teenager, but *big*, stepped directly in front of me like a human wall. "Hello, brother," he rumbled, while his friends closed in, tightening the circle around me. This is right out of a John Wayne movie, I thought miserably.

The large one in front spoke. "You want to smoke the peace pipe with us?"

I remembered from countless Westerns that when the Indians request you share their peace pipe, you share their peace pipe. "Sure, I'd be *delighted,*" I said, desperately hoping that I was coming off as cheerful and hip. Grabbing the pipe, I took a big hard drag.

The taste was bitter and cottony, like sucking on dried, rotten olives. Whatever these Indians had was a dud, but at least it wasn't pot. Aside from a possible case of bad breath, I felt I was home-free.

The pipe then circled the group and, shortly before it was my turn again, the nerves at the base of my neck signalled me that I was about to blast off. I started smacking my lips and swallowed as if I were thirsty. Then the wretched-smelling pipe was in front of me again. As I gingerly took another hit, the Indians stared at my every move. My second puff did not have the delayed reaction of the first. The smoke had discovered my brain's express lane and I felt the earth move under my Gucci loafers.

"Hey," one of them said to another, "he likes our peyote!"

These guys aren't going to bother me now, I thought to myself, relieved. And that was approximately the last coherent thought I had for quite a while. In the time I had had a few more pipe hits, my ominous-looking friends were drifting one by one back into the darkness of the surrounding forest and I was faced with the long, solitary walk home.

How I made it, I'll never know. As I gazed upward, the stars and the white-hot quarter moon seemed to be vibrating as if a hundred Sinatra fireworks shows had exploded at once. The evening chill I had felt walking to the bar seemed to have disappeared, and I no longer felt the incline of the slope as I headed toward the lodge. They tell me that when I reached the lodge I was babbling, "The Beatles are right! Lucy is indeed in the sky with diamonds."

But "high" points notwithstanding, I was still only a minor bureaucrat who was beginning to take long lunches at the Sans Souci and who was growing increasingly bored with my position. "This job isn't to be for long," I told Pearl Bailey over lunch when she queried about my rather dull new status. I certainly hoped I was right, because the frustrations were getting me down. A person can come up with the best ideas in the world and watch them fade like old newspaper as they pass across one hundred bureaucrats' desks being modified, distilled, rewritten, tagged, folded, and mutilated. By the time your idea or proposal is filtered through, it's two administrations later and you've been put out to pasture anyway! The Department of Commerce may have been able to operate that way, but I couldn't, and I was counting the days until I could afford to say good-bye to my departmental paycheck.

Meanwhile, my social life intensified. I was now entertaining, or being entertained, most weeknights, a regular at all the embassy functions and, with the continued support of Eva and Frank Jameson, throwing a few humdingers of my own.

My phone rang constantly with requests for everything from private White House tours to arranging meetings between newly arrived Red Chinese diplomats and eager American businessmen. Had I not still been a civil servant, I could have made a bundle in P.R.

With the flood of invitations came an equal number of requests for me to serve on this committee or to be a patron to that event. The thousands of worthy causes that bombard Washingtonians yearly can hundred-dollar you to death. What price glory!?

Over the next weeks, I held parties for Marlo Thomas, Lucie Arnaz, Helen Reddy, Rockwell president Bob Anderson, astronauts Gene Cernan and Alan Shepard, and I took a gang by bus to see Eva's opening in *A Little Night Music.* With Zahedi and Bill Cook, I was cochairman of the Opera Ball, one of Washington's better attended fun events, and I lent the house for several Democratic fund raisers, hosted a charity backgammon tournament, sponsored a group of local artists, and held a poolside barbecue for underprivileged children. The *Washington Star* had written, "When Peter Malatesta asks you over to his place, go!" And they were coming.

If this sounds like fun, it was and it wasn't. "Out of sight, out of mind" in Washington happens with a quickness that puts infamous Hollywood to shame. For example, with each new administration, guest lists are updated, and those would-be hosts who are not directly in power must make a renewed effort to stay on top.

At this particular period, I was faced with my own version of social survival. In my new position at Commerce, I certainly didn't qualify as powerful, but I wasn't exactly an outsider, either. With my Sinatra-Agnew ties, I had inaugurated my social life in Washington with the *appearance* of clout, but now I had very little going for me but willpower and imagination. I had to maintain my position as an independent entity by working harder and faster than ever.

I began to see more and more of Pearl Bailey and enjoyed every minute with her. She and Eva Gabor had always been the best of friends, and it was a real treat to have them both at the house. Pearl is an exceptional guest at a party. She's a contributor—full of good humor, lively asides, and a great gift of gab. Through her U.N. assignments and her numerous trips to Washington, she developed a closeness with the Middle Eastern emissaries. Her pets were the Jordanians. Pearl was anxious to take her talent abroad and help with charitable causes whenever she could. Generous with her time and energies, when she wasn't looking out for a Jordanian cause, she'd swing over to Saudi Arabia and pitch in there.

Pearl cohosted a couple of my parties, but not as a stand-up prima donna. She'd arrive early and start enthusiastically to cook. One night she'd whip up a Deep South menu. The next, it would be her version of Italian. No one was allowed in the kitchen during Pearl's preparations, and she was very fussy about that. The only one who dared open the door was our live-in jack-of-all-trades, Rob Rohrer, whom Pearl loved. Rob no longer kept a personal supply of herbs, so they were safe together.

I made another effort to revive my friendship with Sinatra. He was opening at Caesar's Palace in Las Vegas and I had what I thought was a super idea. Obligingly, Frank Jameson arranged for a large private jet to fly out a number of prominent Arab ambassadors—the same crew that Agnew was anxiously courting—as well as a mixed group of other Washingtonians. Before we took off, I made a call to Sinatra's office booking a large table. After all, these Arab emissaries were his friends. He had wined, dined, sung, bantered, and cultivated their friendship carefully, and they thought the world of him.

The day of the flight, Zahedi arrived with a picnic-style ice chest packed with caviar and D.P. As the chartered jet winged its way toward the desert, those aboard were in high spirits. It was a nice tribute to their crooning friend, and they were ready for a big opening.

In fact, everyone had a blast on the plane except me, because I wasn't on it! Still very much in government at the time, rather than face the hassle of a potential conflict of interest, I flew commercially with my drinking buddy Bill Cook. Even so, one of the columnists still wrote that I was on the private plane. But when somebody at

Commerce later tried to make a big deal out of it, the writer retracted the statement.

Caesar's Palace was ablaze with excitement that night—as if Julius himself had returned home from Gaul. It was Gaul, all right. I knew something was wrong the minute we walked in. Our table was terrible, buried in a dark corner. I silently hit the ceiling. Sinatra's office knew exactly where every dignitary within A-bomb range of Vegas was sitting. During the performance, our table—which included Eva and Frank Jameson—was not introduced from the floor as many others were, but I wasn't fully positive that something was seriously wrong until I was handed the bill. That's when I heard the final bell tolling. Heretofore, I had never seen a tab when doing something associated with Sinatra, especially when it involved a tableful of hot-shots on an opening night. This one was an impressive first—$1,100. Naturally, I never dared let on that a bill had been presented. I signed it quickly and thought to myself, "Well, I'm in this far, I might as well go all the way." That night, the last of the big spenders left a $250 tip.

I led the group upstairs to a private party. Frank was as cordial as creme de menthe to my guests, and as icy as aquavit in December to me. We didn't so much as exchange glances. I queried an evasive aide of Frank's as to what the hell was the matter.

"Did you ever take into consideration that Vegas is Jewish territory, and you arrive with an armful of Arabs?" he said.

"Oh, come on," I sighed. "They're not fighting the war in the casinos! What's more, Frank's mind doesn't even work that way."

To this day, I never have gotten to the bottom of whatever it was that bothered Frank. We saw each other a year later in a Palm Springs restaurant. It was a fleeting moment. Two rather cold "hellos" and a smile from Barbara, by then his wife. Well, as his song goes: "That's life! Riding high in April, shot down in May!"

I began paying more attention to my growing friendship with Tongsun Park. Perhaps as a result of our bachelor party of the previous year, Tongsun seemed to find me a lively addition to his dinner table. He traveled a great deal and, when in town, entertained with a slightly stodgy, but obviously expensive, touch. He held many parties, but I often thought them too formal, too full of old upper-crusters who bolstered the host's credibility but sometimes bored his perkier guests. Seated between "Old Admiral So-and-So" and "Retired General Ho-Hum," I thought some of his dinners would last forever. But Tongsun was still learning.

In early March, Virginia Page sold the 24th Street house to the Embassy of Cyprus, and it was time to move. Venturing into the real estate listings, I found that for half the amount of rent we were putting into 24th Street, we could lease a beautiful five-bedroom fieldstone home on seven wooded acres in nearby McLean, Virginia. The Jamesons liked the idea, so we moved in.

The house sat on a ridge above the Potamac River, twenty minutes from Washington and a continent away at the same time. With Elliot Richardson and Ted Kennedy for neighbors, I thought the McLean house would be ideal for the particular kind of entertaining that I wanted to do. As come-as-you-are as the city house was, this new Shangri-la really gave my guests the feeling they were in the country, and the parties Eva and I planned reflected that mood.

Tongsun became a regular in McLean and looked forward to our barbecues and spaghetti suppers. Our trees, squirrels, and river view counterpointed his almost daily agenda of black-tie sit-downs, which he hosted in his mansion and in the formal, elegantly private George Town Club, which he owned. Out in McLean, he, like everyone else, kicked off his shoes and watched the river flow.

The traditional last blast in the 24th Street house was, in fact, a birthday party for Tongsun Park. The following year, his birthday was celebrated again in McLean, as was his birthday in 1976. By 1977, he would be *persona non grata,* and when I would try to give him a party in 1978, the FBI would not even allow him to be seen in public, let alone to go to Malatesta's for a birthday celebration.

But that was still in the future. All I could see now, as my friendship with Park grew, was that he was a slick operator. Initially, I was impressed with him because he backed up his megabucks with a shrewd sense of what made business ideas work. He was intrigued by my plan to create a private club and was receptive to meeting Wyatt Dickerson. To use the old cliche, they became like two peas in a pod shortly after they met. Aside from the matter of my club, Dickerson and Park went on to make a number of deals together that were of no concern to me. For starters, Wyatt found a small building which Park bought to house his Washington offices.

Tongsun cornered me at a party one night and asked if I was happy at Commerce. He knew perfectly well that I wasn't and was only waiting for a chance to pursue my club idea. "Keep your eye out for a good location for your club," he said, adding that as soon as I landed a site he would be more than interested in financing it.

That conversation was a green light if ever I saw one. Here was a friend willing to back my idea, and I wasted no time in taking him up on it. But I couldn't help wondering what Park really wanted from me. While he cultivated countless other government contacts, Park never asked me for a single favor. Even though I was well connected in the halls of bureaucracy and Congress, he had never even asked me to use my position for any specific introductions. Of course, traveling in the right party circles in Washington can lead anyone to whomever they may want to know; so to that extent my parties may have been useful to him in a general way, but he didn't really need *me* to meet people. What didn't occur to me at the time was that he may have needed my house—a place where he could meet certain people apparently by accident rather than by design.

The bulk of 1974 was a quiet period. In some ways, the estate in McLean was too relaxing, and for a few fleeting months I was content to attend more parties than I hosted. This was a breather and an escape from the pulse of entertaining in Washington. Actually, too much so! Eva grew restless in the country, Frank found he didn't have to be in Washington as much as he had planned, and after a few months they gracefully cancelled out of the McLean house and concentrated on their life in L.A.

Our parting was amiable, and as I wasn't entertaining much anyway, I didn't feel left on a ledge. Absorbing the other half of the rent merely meant readjusting my budget.

I hosted exactly two people for Thanksgiving 1974—Roz Russell and her husband, Freddie Brisson. Rosalind was by this time slowly growing weaker and not up to a Malatesta extravaganza. The McLean house was exceptionally beautiful in autumn as the thick woods around it exploded with color. The three of us laughed away a quiet afternoon.

It was the last time I ever saw her.

My salary was adequate to sustain the trappings of a good lifestyle, although the parties I was now hosting lacked the endless cases of Dom Perignon of former times. But it didn't matter. In fact, it wasn't much noticed. Once a reputation is established, one can sail for a while on a little wind. Guests at the new house really didn't seem to care that they were being served a nice dry California white wine instead of something regally French.

In lieu of an expensive caterer, I tried large-scale take-out Chinese food, which cost much less. My thrift produced some unexpected results. Instead of gossiping, my guests thought it was terribly clever to go Chinese, since egg rolls and moo-shu pork were strangers to the buffet tables of Washington. "Everybody's bored with caviar," said my friend Buffy Caffritz, "but this dim-sum is sensational!"

My club hunting continued with intense energy now that Park was behind me. Late in the year, I stumbled across a place in the center of Georgetown that I thought would be a knockout, but everyone else took a hell of a lot of convincing. Located in the basement of a former car showroom that was now a parking ramp, The Sundown was nothing more than a second-rate ginmill.

The place had tried everything, and the mood changed nightly. It was a mixed, swinging singles bar during the week, then switched to a white, male gay bar on Saturdays, and then to a predominantly black, mixed-type bar on Sundays, but the manager just couldn't make it work.

I discovered that the owner of the building was a friend of mine. When we sat down to talk business, he was delighted. "I'd love to have you in there," he said. As I unfolded the club idea, I could see he was excited and ready to go.

I went back and talked to Tongsun. We stopped in at the club a brief time later and, after mentally stripping away the Sundown's tacky trappings, we realized its potential. With an M Street location, we thought we had a winner. I contacted my friend Tom Boggs, a corporate law whiz kid and son of the late House majority leader Hale Boggs, to draw up the necessary papers. It wasn't until spring of 1975 that the idea became fact, floated by Park's hefty $400,000 contribution as majority stockholder.

I designed a membership formula by breaking up the city of Washington into forty circles of influence, some of which overlapped and others which never touched. My theory was that, if the club could entice the city's prime movers in each of the business and government circles, the rest would fall into place. I knew that with my contacts the club would see enough Hollywood types and Capitol Hill honchos to make it the bright nightspot that I felt Washington dearly needed.

As I pondered my handwritten rosters of prospective members, I soon found myself facing that well-known—but always unspoken—consideration, the formulation of "A" and "B" lists. Every Washington host or hostess knows about this, as do the admissions committees of all the better clubs. In social Washington, it is everybody's shameful secret, impossibly snobbish, never to be avowed, absolutely essential.

The "A" list, of course, contains the names of people who are currently "in"—the powerful, famous, or rich, whom party-givers consider the best catches, both because they reflect well on their hosts and because their presence will attract other desirable guests.

But since "A's" are much in demand (they seldom accept first-time invitations from non-"A's"), realistic party-givers have to pad out their guestlists with "B's"—those people whom you always expect to see at parties, who certainly always move in the right circles, but whose presence adds no *special* luster to an occasion. The "B's" constitute the indispensable background against which the "A's" are displayed. Working out the right ratios of "A's" to "B's," balancing their personalities, figuring out the proper settings for them, and so on are central to the art of party-giving.

This is central, too, to making up the membership list of a private club. Of course, I had my own definite ideas about who should be rated "A" or "B," but I wanted to check my opinions against those of other D.C. hosts and hostesses. So I got on the phone and began asking indiscreet questions.

The results would have been funny if they hadn't been so frustrating. A few people claimed that they'd never even heard of the "A-B" system. (I reminded them that if they hadn't, the White House certainly had.) Most of the rest acknowledged that they knew about the system, assumed everyone else used it, but swore they'd never dream of employing such cold-blooded and discriminatory criteria in making up their own guestlists. A few social secretaries at some of the embassies went so far as to admit that they actually used "A-B" lists but wouldn't give me any details: "We'd never actually type out lists like that. We're not crazy, Peter." It seemed that they usually listed everyone and then, against various names, would make discreet little pencil marks, the meaning of which only they understood.

Finally, I discovered that the way to get to the heart of the mystery was to ask people what they thought *other* people's "A-B" lists would be like. That brought a terrific response. Nobody minded talking about someone else's secrets. In fact, there was hardly anything they'd rather have talked about. In no time at all, I had almost more "A-B" information than I could handle; and not unexpectedly, it all boiled down to pretty much the same lists I'd started out with in the first place. Tongsun Park's name, I noted, was a solid "A." It wouldn't be too long before it would hardly qualify as an "F."

Soon thereafter we contacted Parrish-Hadley ("A") in New York, one of the city's best-known and most glamorous interior designers. Besides the simple fact that they were good, it was ideal public relations to have a chic New York outfit renovating the place. From the moment we contacted Albert Hadley, the concept sparked press attention, and I went about locking up the all-important first one hundred members.

My home entertaining during this period was low-keyed, but not forgotten. Lazy Sunday afternoon soirées at McLean needed no invitation. It was an open house of sorts, and people would casually drift in and out without much ceremony. One particular Sunday in October, I invited a young actor whose father had entertained me, John Rubenstein. John had just finished a successful run in *Pippin* on Broadway and was weekending in Washington as a guest of Bill Cook. Idealistic young John was full of harsh, moralistic concepts about the ugliness and sorrow of Watergate. While he was expounding some of these, Cook cut in quickly, saying there was someone in the house who might better address Rubenstein's concerns—John Mitchell. Beleaguered and worn out, the former attorney general and head of CREEP was a good friend and an occasional "drop by" guest.

"You mean he's *here*?" Rubenstein shuddered. With that, we moved downstairs where John Mitchell sat quietly chatting with a few other friends. There was an instant rapport between Rubenstein and Mitchell, and the two of them rapped with gratifying respect for each other.

A chagrined Rubenstein later told me, "I can't agree with a lot of what the man did, but I've got to say he's a hell of a nice guy. I like him." As usual, a little dialogue can go a long way when people just sit down and talk.

In February 1975, the *Washington Star* published a long article about the "solo stars" of Washington entertainment. The article pointed out that the three major entertainers in Washington during the 1970s were all bachelors. Besides myself, the article included Iran's Ardeshir Zahedi and Alejandro Orfila, at that time the ambassador of Argentina. "The dynamic bachelors," as we were called, were said to be filling the roles once firmly held by Perle Mesta, Gwen Cafritz, and Marjorie Merriweather Post.

Zahedi was rightfully considered the marathon runner of the trio, the man with the inside track on party politics. Formerly married to the Princess Shahnaz, the late shah's daughter, Ardeshir had a choice of either drawing on his own considerable wealth or using the nearly unlimited funds his country willingly provided. Other considerations apart, neither Alejandro nor I could ever hope to compete with him on that score.

Not nearly as flamboyant as Zahedi, Orfila was a diplomat's diplomat. Reserved yet charming, formal but never cold, Alejandro did well on the budget allowed by his government, but scored considerably higher marks for his smaller, privately financed, dinner parties. In a way, Alejandro and I were opposites. Orfila wouldn't host a six-to-eight cocktail-party-cum-buffet if his job depended on it. In contrast, I have yet to host a sit-down, black-tie dinner.

Weeks after the article appeared, NBC was knocking on the door to see if I'd allow one of my upcoming parties to be covered on their network show "Weekend." I had plans already in the works for a bash for Andy Warhol—a party for his new book, *The Philosophy of Andy Warhol: From A to B, and Back Again.*

I didn't tell my guests about the telecast, so as they arrived they were somewhat bewildered by the klieg lights, the wires, microphones, and crew that had overrun the large McLean house. "This is the most garish circus I've ever seen," growled one senator's wife as her husband not-so-subtly jockeyed for a center spot in front of the camera. "I'm appalled," said another as he waited at the bar for his third scotch.

"Is this a typical Washington party?" Warhol joked as senators Jacob Javits, John Tunney, and Ed Brooke were whirled past in the crowd surging toward the Chinese buffet.

"Definitely," I replied into the microphone of his tape recorder.

"This is all unreal, Peter. It's like a movie," Andy said. At that moment, flamboyant and bejeweled Martha Reed, a socialite with long red hair and chains of pearls, flowed by. "I'm Martha Reed from New York, Paris, and Monte Carlo," she said to Andy. "Doesn't Peter throw the most divine parties in the whole wide world?" Andy turned off his little machine and fled to a quiet corner.

Zahedi, as usual, was in attendance, banked by the press and unafraid to flirt with a pretty woman, even if it was Clare Crawford, the show's host, on camera! The party, with buffet and orchestra in the upper-level living room, and disco-dancing in the lower one, was a bit too much by most Washington standards, but this was what my party reputation was based on, and who was I to let my friends down.

And anyway, I had reason to celebrate: I had just resigned my position at Commerce in anticipation of the opening of my private club. I knew that there would be many, many more gatherings like this, but now they would be held at the club and done for a living.

Following the TV bash, Andy invited me to join him and his "family" for lunch at the Sans Souci. It was fun with a friendly, but unmemorable discussion. After we had eaten, I suggested that we have a little cognac.

He said, "Oh no, I can't have it in a glass."

I didn't question that, but then he leaned over and said, "But I can have it in a coffee cup."

I thought, There it is again. His "public." Andy does not see himself with the image of sitting around after lunch sipping cognac in a crystal snifter, but a cup is okay.

Later in New York, I went through Andy's "Factory," his plant where most of his efforts are turned out, both on paper and on canvas. It's a well-run, very loyal and efficient organization. There's no question that Andy has his followers. When he makes a move, they move. When you invite Andy Warhol for dinner, he'll arrive with at least ten other people. And that's if he comes to Washington: If dinner's in New York, you might have more. Andy was generous to me and made a gift of an original photo-silkscreen of Richard Nixon which he thoughtfully signed—on the back.

I remember asking him once about one of his paintings in the Museum of Modern Art, a painting of a roll of dollar bills. "Andy," I said, "I love the piece, but why the subject of money? How did that come about?"

He said that he had been very excited when he was first asked by the museum for a work. "I asked one of my friends what subject matter I should use, and he said, 'Andy, pick the first thing that comes into your head.' The first thing that came into my head is exactly what I created."

As the club's interior neared completion, we found ourselves head scratching for a name. Our club was modeled, at least in theory, after Doubles in New York and Annabel's in London. Early nominations for our bannerhead included "Matches" (too common), "Capers" (too risque), and "Guv'ner's," which we almost went with until columnist Rowland Evans convinced us it was too confusing in a political town. "Players" was over-used, as was "Aquarius." Then, while I was dining with a friend at a Georgetown restaurant, I noticed a menu heading—"Pisces"—that intrigued me. *Pisces.*

From the restaurant, I called a friend, Hal Gould, who writes a syndicated astrological column. He told me the name "Pisces" was perfect! "It's the sign that combines the moods and mores of all the other signs," he said. To me, that symbolized the overall spirit of the club.

Parrish-Hadley had designed Pisces to make the visitor forget that the club was in a basement. Upon entering, one descended a massive, free-standing curved staircase, which appeared to be a bridge winding over an indoor lagoon. This pool was fed by a two-story slate waterfall that made a dramatic entrance. As the water cascaded over the slate, built-in red light beams crisscrossed the curtain of water. The staircase led to a cocktail lounge, dominated by a long saltwater fish tank behind the main bar. The art in the bar ranged from colorful Robert Mangold lithographs to monochromatic Gene Davis line studies. The carpet that stretched throughout all the rooms of the club was custom-made in Ireland—an exotic, flat-grey wool with coral-colored reefs in scattered patterns.

From the cocktail lounge, one could either proceed into the library and backgammon area or step down into the dining room. The library-backgammon side had white English wingchairs counter-pointed by an abstract Sam Gilliam canvas. The library itself was lined in beige linen drapery, bookcases, and old English prints.

The dining room's focal point was a dance floor flanked by a 1,000-gallon saltwater fish tank, six feet wide and four feet high. With a playful pair of sand sharks dodging the blowfish and moray eel in a white coral reef setting, the turquoise tank set off the deep maroon colors chosen for the massive room. The pillars supporting the building above us were sheathed in mosaics that reflected the candlelight and the crystal service. Long, deep red banquettes surrounded the room and made for cozy *tête-à-têtes.*

Another dining room was reserved for private parties. It was lined with huge black-and-white Warhol flowers against red walls and had its own entrance onto a side street.

Our secret list of founding members contained 100 names. Among them were David Brinkley; Douglas Kiker; Robert Strauss; Anna Chennault; Governor Earle Clements; Vic Gold; Arthur Goldberg; senators Barry Goldwater, Ed Brooke, and Vance Hartke; Chuck and Lynda Robb; John Warner; the Bob Hopes; J. Carter Brown; Bryce Harlow; Frank Sinatra; Pearl Bailey; Gregory Peck; Eva Gabor; Sol Linowitz; Winthrop Rockefeller; Alejandro Orfila; the ambassadors of Saudi Arabia, Jordan, the United Arab Emirates, China, Argentina, Mexico, Syria, and, of course, Ardeshir Zahedi.

So much for the founders. The club then set its membership roster into three categories: resident members (local socialites); nonresident members (senior diplomats, the Congress, and hot out-of-towners); and special members (attractive young professionals under thirty-two). Membership fees varied from $600 down to $150, depending upon which berth one fit into. The only honorary member was Walter Washington, mayor of the District of Columbia.

In many respects the RM's, NRM's, and SM's were the most important members. Their almost nightly support would be a must if the club were going to make a go of it. Drawing from my now elaborately expanded dossier, I found a sizable number of locals ready and eager to join. But as they say, you win some, you lose some.

Pisces was proud to have Bill and Buffy Cafritz sign up, along with the Mandy Ourismans and Mrs. Forest Mars (as in candy bars). Alas, with the years finally taking their toll, spunky Alice Roosevelt Longworth, one of my all-time favorites, politely declined. I felt anyone from the influential Kennedy Center crowd could be invaluable, especially with the glamorous opening-night and after-theater dinners I knew they'd host. When Kennedy Center director Roger Stevens, along with PR man Pierre Franz Chapou and patroness Ina Ginsburg joined, I felt the bases there were well-covered.

Obviously, Pisces wanted publishing magnate Katharine Graham, not only for her sparkling self, but because her membership would have a shepherd-effect on the bright circle around her. It didn't work, and perhaps for that reason we never did recruit Art Buchwald, Ben Bradlee, Sally Quinn, the Joe Alsops, Henry and Muffie Brandon and their likes. But we were fortunate in being able to round up several numbers from the "other" paper, *The Washington Star:* copublisher Jack Kauffmann and his wife, Patsy, and managing editor Sid Epstein and his influential wife, fashion editor Eleni.

It always bothered me that so many other Washington clubs excluded Jewish members, and I certainly didn't intend to follow suit. Some advisers on our membership committee cautioned me about mixing high-profile Arab ambassadors with leaders of the Jewish community, but I thought that was a crock! I proceeded to invite drugstore tycoon Sheldon Fantle and his merry wife, Jerri; stirred it up even more by inviting Fantle's major competitor, Robert Haft; and then added meat-supplier socialite Bernie Goldstein and hardware king John Hechinger. All graciously accepted, and when we finally landed the owner of the prestigious Madison Hotel, Marshall Coyne, I knew this circle was golden.

Another circle that needed to be well-represented in Pisces was the city's black leadership. In addition to Mayor Washington, Pisces invited Dr. LaSalle Lefall of Howard University; Sterling Tucker, the chairman of the City Council; Bob Washington, the head of the Democratic party in D.C.; and Bill Fitzgerald, one of the city's most powerful bank presidents. Fitzgerald's bride, Tina, would often be said to be the most beautiful woman in the club, and early in the game one of my waiters would get all hot and bothered after mistaking her for Ali MacGraw. In a city infamous for socially slighting blacks, I found this circle to be one of the most glamorous and exciting available.

Besides excluding the working press, we wanted to avoid accepting other restaurateurs as members. They were welcome to *visit* as my personal guests but, on the whole, I thought having competitors in the general membership a bad idea. Washingtonians dine out often and grow close ties to many establishment owners. I didn't want any guests feeling guilty about eating at Pisces because some competitor of mine was present. Besides, many restaurateurs are often like many congressmen; they aren't necessarily the classiest guys around.

The only way Pisces would become a lively night spot would be to make sure that its membership ranks contained plenty of young, under 32 live wires. Otherwise, Pisces could turn out to be just another opulent, dull, upper-crusty club, where the complexions blended in with the bathroom tile. These "kids," even more carefully selected than their seniors, would make the older members feel more youthful; by the same token, for the young hotshot on the way up, Pisces was a unique place to tip a few with some pillars of the establishment.

Burton B. Hanbury, Jr., John Ford, and Jamie Kabler looked more like soccer players in tuxes than rising young legal stars. Pretty, aristocratic Naila Al-Soyowel and her enterprising brothers, offspring of the Saudi Arabian ambassador, exuded dignified fun. Howard Joynt, Georgetown's most flamboyant playboy, would bring his antics into the club, and Robert Haft, Jr., who parleyed a family loan into a nationwide bookstore chain by the age of twenty-five, would often dance the night away. These "youngsters," already making the social pages, were followed by a hand-picked variety of younger White House and Diplomatic Corps "juniors," all of whom had a penchant for entertaining.

Washington's older bachelors and bachelorettes were also an important group. I felt that it was essential that singles feel welcome and comfortable at the bar. While I certainly didn't want Pisces to be thought of as a place where pick-ups were possible, I wasn't averse to cultivating a little of that atmosphere of romance that only singles can create.

Some of Pisces's early free spirits included Patrick Daly, assistant chief of protocol for the State Department; Steve Martindale; congressmen Sonny Montgomery, David Bowen, and Larry Pressler; Ashland Oil troubleshooter Harry Williams; and TV personality Deena Clark. For the foreign connection, we added Hani Masri, a handsome Arab importer-exporter and His Excellency, Saeed Ghobash, from the United Arab Emirates, and the youngest ambassador in Washington.

From the debutante circle, we captured Standard Oil heiress Page Lee Hufty; former ambassador Joseph Farland's daughter, Brooke; and Getty heiress Deecy Stevens.

Some, released from the bonds of marriage by death or decree, were eager for memberships. Tandy Dickinson had a natural "in" due to her constant companionship with Tongsun Park. Rose Marie Bogley, a very wealthy young widow from the horsey set of Middleburg, was considered the ultimate catch by many interested black-

tiers. Aldus Chapin, a liberated cave dweller, provided just the right touch of elite acceptance. And what would a group of well-to-do singles in Washington be without the ubiquitous Bill Cook, forever holding his double Cutty on the rocks and his pack of Winstons?

With an assembled fleet of tuxedoed waiters, two maitre d's, doormen, car valets, bartenders, coat checkers, busboys, a social secretary, a chef and a dozen kitchen staff, a disc jockey, and even a professional fish feeder, Pisces was ready to swing into action by December of 1975.

A week or so before opening, Tongsun invited me to join him and Tandy for a few restful days at his hideaway in the Dominican Republic. He was on the phone the better part of the afternoon of our arrival, and by the afternoon of the second day, Tandy and I had hardly seen him. We had spent our time on the beach and tennis court. Tandy was great company, full of warmth, but often lonely even with Tongsun in the next room. Apparently, Tongsun intended to use this jaunt as a working trip, so I said to Tandy, "Enough is enough! I'll be back later. We're going to have some fun, and he's coming with us!"

I went out and chartered a luxury fishing boat with crew. It was time to get my friend away from his papers for at least half a day. I rented fishing gear and stocked the boat with fresh fruit, sandwiches, soft drinks, and beer. We lured TSP (the name his intimates called him) on board and took off for a cove with a secluded beach. When we got there, I jumped in for a swim and finally convinced Tongsun to take off his bathing suit and swim naked, something I'm sure he had never done before. We frolicked around like porpoises in that diamond blue water, while Tandy sat back and laughed at the two of us. She said we were like two little boys swimming in their favorite fishing hole. I think Tongsun really loved this kind of freedom, but he seldom went so far in letting his hair down—much less his pants!

In mid-December, Pisces opened with a series of three parties. The first was a press preview reception with invitations going to the local and national media. This was done to placate the social writers, who were not allowed to become members as long as they were working press. In order to preserve the credentials of a socially exclusive club, press access had to be limited and funneled ideally through just one source. The old rule of supply and demand applies as much to the dissemination of inside gossip as it does to economics. If

Pisces were destined to be the new "in" spot, to the extent that we limited inside information we would be able to arouse curiosity.

It was a good plan and it worked well as we approached opening night. But with human nature as it is, Wyatt Dickerson became increasingly sensitive toward my growing public identity with Pisces. I could understand the frustration he must have felt at perpetually being referred to as "Mr. Nancy Dickerson," and now he had the burden of being thought of as Malatesta's silent partner, but I thought his sensitivity was misplaced. After all, I had been chosen for my professional role by Park, largely *because* of the heavy press attention that was already following me around. But Wyatt resented the club being referred to as "Peter's place," and it was downhill between us from then on.

The second event given by the club was a black-tie dinner dance for 140 given by two of Washington's most endearing socialites, Bill and Buffy Cafritz. Besides being close friends, the Cafritzes were very supportive of the club concept and were promised the first party after the opening-night gala. They took it as an honor and hosted a memorable and elegant affair.

Buffy had invited a galaxy of blue-chip ambassadors and wealthy socialites who later joined the club as a result of her party. Feting Jacques Rouet, the president of Christian Dior, the Cafritzes lent immediate establishment acceptance to our fledgling operation. They were so interested in a good show, it was necessary to hire a guard to protect the sterling silver service for 140 that Buffy lent the club that night.

For the third night, the club hosted founding members with a cocktail buffet. Most of the original 100 appeared, and I would have predicted a flawless evening except that we still hadn't even received our liquor license!

Finally, at 5:30 that night, as we were about to open to the membership on a regular basis, the license appeared by messenger just moments before I was about to start giving away drinks . . . again! But as the members poured down the stairs and staff scurried to greet them, I found myself in a state of euphoria. Not because the damn license arrived, but because I now finally felt that my dream had come true. From a tiny idea in the back of my head, to chatter over lunch, to a damp basement, to a glittering half-million-dollar private playpen,

Pisces had become a reality. It didn't matter that night that even with Park's money the club was $80,000 in the red from cost overruns. It didn't matter that Dickerson glared at me as I patted backs and shook hands. It didn't matter that I was so tired I could have curled up on our banquettes at a moment's notice. My idea had worked, and I would have passed out cigars like a proud father except that the only ones I had were Cuban, a gift from a non-aligned ambassador, and why raise eyebrows?

Chapter Nine

From its first days, Pearl Bailey was gung ho about the club. Taking a small table for two in a corner banquette near the stairs, Pearl trademarked herself with an elegant silver champagne bucket containing only a single bottle of cold Heineken. Accessible and gregarious to anyone walking in, Pearlie Mae was a spontaneous ringleader whenever the Force was with her, which was most of the time. In appreciation, I installed a brass plaque on the wall behind her.

At that time, the Hustle was being danced by practically everyone but the upper echelons of Washington. Pearl caught on to it quickly and one night during a dinner dance in her honor she corralled all within earshot for a spontaneous lesson, taught only as Pearl could. It was the kind of happening that spreads news around gossipy Georgetown faster than a Hill scandal.

Among Pearl's willing recruits that night were Elizabeth Taylor, Lucie Arnaz, Eva Gabor, and the ambassadors of Jordan, Iran, Israel, and Egypt. The music cranked up and Pearl formed two lines of dancers. Though the selection was arbitrary at first, the less coordinated soon found themselves consigned to Pearl's "B"-list. Elizabeth Taylor was the first casualty. "Honey," Pearl bellowed, "you gotta get in the back row 'til you learn how to move that. . . . You know what I mean, honey!" It had to be the first time in Taylor's life that she was ever put in the back row of anything, but everyone roared.

A few nights later, Elizabeth Taylor again appeared with her escort for the evening, Bicentennial Director John Warner. It was a slow weekday and very late. Although most of the supper crowd had cleared out, Liz and John took a quiet corner table in the back. Mellow and pleasant after a long evening, the couple wanted something to eat but didn't know just what. The conversation seesawed until Liz chirped that she really only wanted an ice-cream soda.

That was easier said than done, since my kitchen staff had long since punched out for the night. After rattling around in the pantry, I finally appeared with a cold volcano of fudge sauce and Haagen-Dazs, borrowed a few slivered almonds normally tossed onto sautéed trout. Gazing over my masterpiece, Liz and John cooed and held hands like a two-straw teenage couple in a malt shop.

In a way, that little incident was typical of Pisces. The club was an extension of my living room, and whether it was a celebrity with the munchies or an up-and-coming dance coach, my guests comfortably did whatever they wanted. Despite its trappings and its ever-growing membership, it was the sense of familiarity that made the club. It was like every night was a party at Peter's.

Like any fledgling operation, Pisces had its share of bugs to iron out. The kitchen's performance record was a bit spotty. Our Italian chef had come from an excellent small restaurant which was accustomed to handling effortlessly thirty to forty dinners during an evening. Now he was responsible for organizing a staff of eight and preparing twice as many nightly dinners. The results were sometimes erratic, and some picky eaters like Zahedi began to be more conspicuous in the bar than in the dining room.

By April, Pisces was ready for Andy Warhol. In celebration of our large collection of his works, I hosted a party in his honor which he attended with actresses Monique Van Vooren and Carol Lynley. Monique was wrapped in a black mink halter top that shocked some of the members, but not as much as Andy's blue jeans and sneakers—two insurmountable taboos of the strict Pisces dress code. Before you could blink, a rather snooty young lawyer was on my back. "How come *he* can wear blue jeans in here and I can't?"

"Listen," I said defensively, "when you can get 80K for a can of Campbell's soup, I'll let you wear blue jeans too." But the following day, the local gossip mill had a ball reporting about Warhol being allowed in that way.

There were other awkward moments. As I've said, I had a policy from the beginning that the owners of other first-class restaurants were welcome to enjoy an evening at Pisces as my personal guests. This perpetuated a pleasant business rapport and it was a gesture of repayment for all the good tables and on-the-house bottles of champagne I had been given. Duke Ziebert, a colorful sportsman-owner of a very popular downtown restaurant, arrived unannounced one night and my doorman buzzed me, "Duke's here with a date." I signalled a quick okay.

It was a busy evening with the bar and dining room packed, but the word flashed within seconds: Liz Ray was in the club! The Wayne Hays exposé was in full gear and the not-so-subtle murmurs were flying. "What's going on?" "What the hell is Peter thinking of?" "I don't believe it!"

Seating the couple at a nice table, I exchanged pleasantries with my two old friends. Duke's food had kept me overweight for years, and Liz had been a guest at my parties when I first came to town. A likable, down-to-earth gal, no one had known or cared what she did on her own time. While at my parties, she had been a lively conversationalist and had conducted herself in a ladylike manner.

With some of the members getting increasingly uptight and Liz and Duke feeling no pain, I decided that offense was the only possible defense. Making a beeline for the disc jockey booth, I selected a hot hit of the day—"Shame, Shame, Shame"—and played it good and loud, completely out of context with the dinner music it interrupted. Laughter and short applause rippled through the room, and Liz, who's weathered a lot more than a frisky DJ, took her date by the arm, got up, and danced.

Through Andy Warhol and Monique Van Vooren, I had become acquainted with the great Rudolf Nureyev and enjoyed spending time with him. One day, Monique came to me for a favor—Rudi wanted to meet Henry Kissinger. Although confidential tête-à-têtes were hardly uncommon at any of my gatherings, I steered away from deliberately setting up a party format that was solely designed to put any two heavyweights together. I always kept a varied number of different ingredients in my social stew, but for Rudi I bent a few of my own rules and organized a party at the club that would put the dancer at the elbow of Kissinger during dinner. At the time, there was no other informal way for Nureyev to get together with the very busy Secretary of State.

In Rudi's case, the cause was an honorable one; he was willing to do anything possible to get his parents out of the Soviet Union. While ostensibly a birthday for Monique, it was actually Rudi's day in court with the only man who could possibly help. I'm not sure if their dinner chatter amounted to anything productive for the elder Nureyevs, but at least Rudi was able to take his best shot.

Later that evening, with politics, a little veal, and some champagne under his belly, Rudi was anxious to see the late night life in Washington, so we walked around Georgetown and ducked into a few bistros. I thought he would be amused by the east side of town, a warehouse area interspaced with discos and clubs. The most jumping places were the gay, or bisexual, dance halls. He seemed willing to explore that end of town, so I took him to a place called The Lost and Found, which has a considerable amount of livewire action. He pulled his cap down and flipped up the collar of his jacket, saying, "I'd just like to go in there and see what's happening. No one will recognize me."

I said, "Fine. We'll take a look."

We went in for three minutes and, in that short time, the word buzzed all over this extravagant disco that Nureyev was there.

"Well, Rudi, we can do one of two things," I said. "We can get the hell out of here, which is the best idea in the world right now, or we can have a few drinks and read all about it in the *Post* tomorrow. If we stay, at least I can say I danced with Nureyev!"

He chuckled at that and suggested we turn on our heels and try someplace less high-profile. But sure enough, I had a call in the morning from a popular local gossip columnist who wanted to know if it was true that . . . . I have never lied to the press, so I said, "There are a lot of people in town who look a lot like us. On the other hand, for just doing a tour of the city, it's hardly worth the press, don't you think?" Thank God she was in a good mood that day and the subject was dropped.

Besides Rudi and Andy, a number of Manhattanites enjoyed using the club, but none as much as my friend Martha Reed. As a non-resident member, she was, and is, a charming character few could forget. I dare anyone ever to estimate the worth of her jewelry collection. Every night she came in with another array of large, spectacular stones that she seemed to take as much for granted as popcorn at a matinee. Martha deserved the finest gems because she's one herself. Elegant, but lighthearted, men found it easy to think of her as a good pal. Among the women, she was regarded as somewhere between Mata Hari and Mme. de Pompadour.

Pisces' grand curving staircase proved to be an irresistible entrance maker with a built-in audience in the cocktail lounge. Martha prided herself on being one up on any of the other women in town and, although it was a warm spring night, she once arrived at the club wrapped in a new, floor-length sable coat.

"Sweetheart, do you want me to check this for you?" I said, automatically signalling the coat concierge to come running.

"Don't be ridiculous," she said. "I didn't buy it to *check* it!"

Aghast, I said, "What the hell are you going to do with it?"

"Watch!"

Carefully draped over one shoulder, the coat "carelessly" dragged on the steps behind her as she walked down with a calculated look of total indifference. She had the undivided attention of some men and every woman in the place.

On another occasion in Manhattan, Martha and I were sipping bubbles at El Morocco in silent misery. Sinatra was performing that weekend and, as much as we wanted to see his show, tickets were impossible to buy. Even the scalpers were empty-handed. As we commiserated, I noticed Mickey Rudin huddled with business associates at another table. Martha was wearing a solitaire diamond on her hand which, if you looked at it quickly, might have been mistaken for a small, upside-down glass ashtray.

"Let me have your ring, dear," I asked.

"What?" she said, almost oblivious to the question.

"Let me have your ring."

"Peter dear . . ."

"Just let me have the ring. I'll give it right back."

Thinking I was slightly insane, she took it off and I wrapped it in a napkin and dashed off a note. Then I called over Angelo, the headwaiter, and asked that it be delivered to Mr. Rudin.

Dear Mickey,
I'm having a hell of a time getting tickets for Frank's opening. It seems they are as scarce as diamonds. Perhaps we can barter six for this??

Rudin was typically preoccupied with his conversation and

abstractly glanced only at the note as a loud clank hit his butter dish. Rudin's companions stared in disbelief as he looked around and caught my wink.

Ten minutes later, we got the ring back, along with the tickets. "Oh, Peter," Martha groaned with her hand on her chest. "You've got some nerve! I haven't even insured this one yet!"

Martha's colorful presence was typical of the easygoing atmosphere I tried to encourage at Pisces. One night, Gregory Peck and Kirk Douglas came in with their respective entourages of family and friends. They were celebrating a birthday of one of Peck's children, and when last-call time rang in at 2:00, I had a worried maitre d' on my hands. The Peck pack was drinking Dom Perignon like it was going out of style. "What do I do?" my captain asked me.

"Keep pouring it!"

"But, but . . ." he stuttered.

"Don't disturb their evening. They're having a ball, and anyway, from now on they're *my* guests."

They drank until 4:00. I can't say I made any financial profit from their presence, but all the press noted was the fact that they were there.

Running past curfew did not happen frequently, but when it was necessary to bend a few rules, I usually did so without regret. But we had a couple of close calls. One particular evening, a number of prominent senators were being wined and dined by a member. Although it was well after closing time, this party continued to chat and joke over cognac. Among the guests was Senator Hubert Humphrey, animated and obviously enjoying the seclusion of the club. He was full of amusing stories and no one at their table was really aware that it was past closing time, so I decided to leave them alone. I told the doorman and support staff to lock up anyway, and I'd "sit" for them. By that time, 3:00 had rolled around.

The phone at the bar buzzed, and my off-duty doorman was in a panic. "I've got a cop at the door and he wants in, Mr. Malatesta. Now what?" he whispered.

"Stall him for a minute. I'll be right up," I said, concealing a mild panic of my own. This was all I needed. Pisces busted on the liquor laws with no less than three U.S. senators, including the very popular Humphrey, implicated. "Wyatt's going to love this," I thought as I scurried into the dining room, my mind filled with the image of a well-publicized paddy wagon whisking us all away. Keeping the tone of my voice nonchalant, I informed the guests at the table that it was very late and that the main entrance was locked. Would they mind leaving by the rear door near the alley . . . immediately? I felt as if I were clearing out a speakeasy during Prohibition.

As the ladies gathered up their wraps and the men finished their drinks and concluded their stories, the phone in the dining room buzzed. The doorman said the police officer was getting irate because he was being detained at the top of the stairs. Perhaps the senators got wind of the second call, because they left without much more than a glance from me. After seeing them out, I rushed into the lobby and up the stairs with an excuse about being distracted by some "midnight oil" bookwork.

The officer demurely asked if it was possible for him to have a cup of coffee. He was the regular late-shift cop for that particular Georgetown beat, and it was cold outside. He had not been in the club yet, and wanted to introduce himself. As we sat at the bar chatting, he with his coffee and me breathing a deep sign of relief into a brandy snifter, I realized the guy couldn't have cared less whether or not I still had a roomful.

After that, he was welcomed into the club for coffee any time. And when I finally told him what had happened before he came downstairs, he only laughed. "I just wanted to see if your coffee was any better than the rest of the joints down the street."

Although the membership was growing fast, Dickerson was becoming more irritable. Constant tidbits of gossip were being leaked about "biggies" visiting the club, and, although I was delighted that my press plants were arousing the imagination of the public, they were also arousing Wyatt's temper. The crisis came when the *Washington Star* published a satirical parody about a "mythical private club called 'The Club Virgo,' " which had an indoor waterfall and tanks full of dangerous fish. The two main characters were a short, talkative fellow named "PeeWee Malajusta" and a slick figure of a man called "Whynot Dixon."

It was an innocent-enough spoof, but then followed another gossip item which was headlined, "Piranha Time at Pisces." "Piranha Time" explained that both of us were now starting to welcome arriving guests and members and asked, "Should each groan like that while the other one is greeting?" Apparently the tension between

Wyatt and me had now become a public spectacle, and neither of us was pleased, with each other or the press.

Vogue magazine helped to soften the squabbling image by writing up the club in its May 1976 issue as the glamor place for party people. But for locals, the feud between Dickerson and me was the only really entertaining cat fight in town.

We didn't have time to dwell on the details of our differences for very long. Tongsun's troubles were bubbling to the surface and our attention now switched to our third partner. It was common gossip that an investigation of Park was about to break loose. Only now did I begin to realize that as far back as the club's planning stages, there had been talk that Park was, so to speak, a disaster waiting for a place to happen.

Most of the current rumors centered on Park's being, or not being, registered as a foreign agent, and I therefore quickly put Tongsun together with attorney Tommy Boggs. Tom warned Park that his activities, both social and commercial, might fall under the jurisdiction of the Foreign Agent Act, and that Park had better give thought to registering, just to be on the safe side. But Tongsun wouldn't hear of it, claiming that he was doing nothing to warrant it. Boggs did his best, considering that the attorney was speaking as a friend and not as Park's counsel.

There was certainly no secret that Tongsun had put up the big bucks for Pisces, but it was also true that Park seldom appeared there. The few times he did were to have a quiet one-to-one dinner with me. The George Town Club was his showcase, and between it and his grandiose home he entertained all Washington as if he owned it, or at least as if he had made a substantial down payment on Capitol Hill. His guests included vice presidents, White House aides, senior members of Congress, cabinet officers, and agency heads. The personable baby-faced Park was like a Hollywood producer summoning actors from central casting to play roles in his production. His guests of honor were usually foreign executives and officials with whom he wished to curry favor for potential deals. What better way to impress them with your power than to have the powerful in attendance? But although Park spent money like he printed it, it never crossed my mind that he might have been involved in anything of the magnitude of Koreagate.

It's one thing to know senators and congressmen, but from a

practical standpoint in Washington, it's liable to be more useful to know their staffs; and part of keeping well-informed involves knowing and socializing with these "kids." So while senators might brush off any comment about Park's alleged difficulties, often his staffers would privately have a lot more to say on the matter. Mainly from them I gathered that Park's trouble was serious, although I still knew no details. But when I tried to convey some of my alarm to Park, he affected not to be very much concerned. Unless he was acting, he was dead wrong.

For the Bicentennial Fourth of July weekend, Pisces pulled out all the stops and arranged for a lavish buffet on its roof. At the time, I was courting a gorgeous model and photographer, Helga Leifeld, whom I had met in California a year or two earlier at Pips, an L.A. private club. We both shared a friendship with Sinatra, and we dated when the mood and location suited us. Helga was my guest for the Fourth of July bash.

Weeks before, we had attended a gala at the Kennedy Center where Helga caught the eye of Alex Orfila, then escorting Jacqueline Onassis for the evening. Alex, as always, was the impeccable diplomat, but even he couldn't stop staring at Helga, who glanced back a few times herself. She told me later that she didn't think Jackie appreciated the innocent flirtation, so no one had a chance to become acquainted. Too bad! Had I known what was ahead, I would gladly have swapped dates.

Helga looked spectacular the night of the rooftop buffet and, knowing my duties as host would keep me hopping, I asked a friend of mine, abstract artist Todd Miner, to keep an eye on her. Todd had an attractive date of his own and, as one of the young members of Pisces, found it hard not to circulate. So there was Helga, alone and wistful, while I shook hands with the throng. When I turned around, who should be purring all over her and grinning like a Cheshire cat, but my dear friend Alex.

A few days later, I received a most proper telephone call from "Ambassador Orfila" who, in a most traditional and gentlemanly way, asked me what my relationship was with Helga. I explained that she was a great pal of mine and that we had shared many a good time together. . . . "But if you're looking for my permission to call her, Alex, consider it done!"

He did, and a year later I found myself the best man at their wedding.

As the summer drew to a close, everybody at Pisces needed a vacation, but I wanted to continue the momentum of club comradery. It occurred to me that if we could take a group of members on a successful and fun trip, we'd have a running start on the fall social season.

I planned a club-sponsored trip to the Algarve region of Portugal for 140 members. There was not a single person on the $399 charter flight (hotel included) who couldn't have afforded to fly first-class to Europe any time they wanted, but the idea of a peer-group junket to an exotic place was irresistible. First in line for the excursion was Alejandro Orfila, soon to be followed by a good many other pillars of the "candlelight community."

The trip to Portugal, in addition to its continual parties and antics, achieved one important unplanned result. Several of the vacationing members were black, and although I was certain that they would be readily accepted into the activities of the others, I couldn't help worrying that they might feel more comfortable going off and doing things by themselves.

Sure enough, two days into the trip, a few black members drifted off on their own and discovered a fabulous fish stand right on the beach. Nothing fancy, but the little shack seemed to have the best smoked fish in the world. They set up their headquarters there and with the help of a little sangria started a party. News of their discovery spread quickly throughout our troop, and from that moment on, any possibility of cliquishness evaporated. Group mingled with group and the result, for the rest of the trip, was one big party.

The friendships that started on that beach with a handful of sardines developed into lasting relationships of business and pleasure between two previously polarized communities. Parties aren't always the frivolous things they seem.

The night of the first sangria bash, Sid Epstein and I were wandering back to our rooms. We stopped at the elevator and waited for what seemed like ages. Staring at the white lights above the door, we patiently kept expecting the light to flash when the elevator finally arrived. Someone a bit more sober walked by and asked us what we were doing. When we told him, he burst out laughing. "That's the sign for the men's room!" he roared. Sid and I were pegged with that by the rest of the gang for years to come. And so it was in Portugal.

For Pisces' big fall kickoff party, I turned again to my friend Alejandro Orfila, who had another of his great ideas. He and his business partner, Turner Reuter, Jr., imported miniature horses from Argentina; tiny spotted things that stood a mere twenty-four inches high and looked like dogs. Named after their breeder, Falabellas, the pint-sized ponies were new to the United States and, we decided, deserved an elegant soirée at Pisces.

The amazing creatures were thoroughly housebroken and so civilized they actually watched TV when hanging around Orfila's country spread in Middleburg, Virginia. Having a flock of them running scot-free throughout the club for an evening was as surreal as a Dali oil. One, named Belief, walked along the length of the bar, stepping so gingerly as not to disturb a single cocktail napkin. Then she stopped and stood gazing at the fish tank as if it were playing a rerun of "Mr. Ed." Turner confided that in between television watching, they practiced their balance by standing around on tabletops back in Middleburg. Someone commented that it was only a matter of time before they appeared in the Neiman-Marcus catalogue.

I delighted in seeing them scamper about, but I still kept a worried eye on our $32,000 carpeting. "Alex, there's enough horseshit around here already!" I bemoaned aloud. I was put at ease when Orfila laughingly explained how the little beauties had all been given enemas by the vet before they got to the door of Pisces.

Later in the month, I again found myself with a flustered call from the doorman about a crasher. "Sir," he explained, "there's a Mrs. Lopez Portillo up here with some other people. What should I do? She's waiting at the top of the stairs, but she's not a member.

I said, "For God's sake, escort her quickly to the bottom of the stairs. She's the wife of the president of Mexico!"

This was actually her second visit. Following her husband's inauguration, the dear lady had been a guest of the ambassador of Mexico for dinner, and on a return trip to Washington took it upon herself to drop by unannounced. She really enjoyed the facilities, and had it not been a breach of protocol, I was sure I could have corralled her into a membership. Instead, I "ate" her bill and chalked it up as P.R.

On another occasion on fairly short notice, I received a call from New York promoter Bobby Zarim to the effect that celebrated body-builder Arnold Schwartzenegger, now an author and movie star, could use a party in Washington to boost his rising fortunes. I reluctantly agreed to put it together at the club, but in the back of my mind I was uncertain whether the membership was ready to toast somebody's muscles.

To my surprise, even the most sophisticated Georgetown cave dwellers, male and female alike, couldn't resist grabbing the forearm or bicep of the basically bashful Arnold. Where I expected haughtiness and a lukewarm turnout, I received a packed cocktail lounge and downright voyeuristic oglers. As Fats Waller used to say, "One never knows, do one?"

With all the accumulated power that could gather in the dark banquettes of the club, it was easy to see how such social yet private facilities would be a field day for exclusive and conveniently obscure business deals. The potential was there from the beginning, and in some respects, it was one of the unspoken reasons for the club's very existence. What the members did at their own table, on their own time, was strictly their affair, and as far as the world was concerned, they were merely at a private restaurant. No one would be privy to anything that went on at the tables, not even the ever-present Peter (or Wyatt). No one, that is, but the hovering, ever-watchful waiters.

The waiters of Pisces were a mixed lot, ranging from middle-aged Germans with families to brash, hot-out-of-college Georgetown youngsters. In between were Iranians, proudly flashing green cards, some highly formal kids from Thailand, and a few Italians fresh off the cruise ships. These guys saw it all, with one eye on the sports cars they all seemed to buy with ease and another looking over their shoulder for the IRS auditor.

There was a regular system of information sharing and after-hours gossip, commonly referred to as the "shift-drink." After closing, the boys would take off their cummerbunds and have a round or two with the boss. I'd listen to all kinds of stories—how this ambassador was really an S.O.B., and that congressman's wife knew all about her husband's date, and so on. It never ceased to amaze me how much the seemingly scurrying waiters really noticed and remembered. They knew that anything they said to the press could cost them their one-man gold mine, but they also knew they had an attentive boss who liked to keep his ear to the ground. In the process, I developed a dossier that even the CIA might envy.

"I couldn't believe it, Peter!" one waiter would say breathlessly. "Chef made a huge portion of linguine and white clam sauce and, you know what, Lee Radziwill ate it all. Every bit! And she cleaned up the juice with her bread. How such a skinny lady could eat all that, I'll never know."

"Margaret Trudeau was in with Steve last night, Peter. She looked kinda plain. I thought she'd look like this big star. All they talked about was what a big hit her book was gonna be."

"Mr. Malatesta! I just can't work with the Secret Service following me around, watching every move I make. What do they think . . . I'm going to put arsenic in the president of Ecuador's crab claws?"

"Umm, that Liz (Taylor) is built! She's 'in' on something to do with that big horse show."

"I'm sorry, sir, but Vincent Price was not at all impressed with his rack-of-lamb. Said it was dry. The nerve! I wanted to tell him to shove it, but then I figured I'd have Frankie Hewitt on my ass!"

"Michael Blumenthal's wife practices Chinese in the bathroom every morning with a tape recorder, and he told his friend he can't *stand* it!"

"Ah, they left us 20 percent on the big Valentino party, but they were so damn fussy it wasn't enough."

"Did you tell Peter about Bill Cook asking Mitch to take Martha Reed's ring in the kitchen and clean it with Windex?"

"Peter, who was that babe Jimmy Connors came in with? His sister, my eye! It looked like love to me."

"Mr. Hariyanto left an entire bottle of Romanee-Conte '69! His girlfriend got sick and they split. This stuff costs $165 bucks. Here, give it a try!"

I heard it all, and then some.

Even on the busiest Saturday night, Pisces consistently tried to maintain its sense of ease and relaxation. It could appear crowded with people, but usually a guest never felt hemmed in. Its sheer size of 12,000 square feet accounted in part for that. So when the Carter Inauguration festivities began in January 1977, no one expected that Pisces, often considered a Republican club, would erupt as it did into a suffocating, three-ring-circus version of a human zoo.

The black-tie stampede started early and, by midnight, when the evening had just begun, we were so overcrowded that women no longer bothered to check their furs. Piles of mink, fox, and ermine were tossed unattended in corners as couples rushed down the stairs, only to reach a hopelessly backed up bar. My main bartender, Jay Sweeney, normally chipper and conversational even when busy, became a cursing, stemware-throwing demon. Drink-splashed waiters hurled themselves into the masses of jubilant Democratic swingers as if the revelers were sandbags. Victory-drunk senators' wives, who are usually catered to like Chinese empresses, were lucky if they got a canapé.

The dress code was in shambles. When Cher and her date Gregg Allman arrived, looking like they were ready for a picnic in Tibet, all I could do was smile and shrug to my doorman. Other guests like Lorne Greene, Jack Nicholson, and Kirk Douglas were dressed more appropriately, but almost went unnoticed by the elbowing throng. And it got worse.

My doorman was in a stupor. When Paul Newman arrived with "Number 2" tycoon Warren Avis, they were promptly turned away for non-membership. Caught in the mob scene downstairs, I was unable to get to the door and the poor guy manning the gangplank, so to speak, didn't know Avis from Hertz. When it flashed all over town that Paul Newman was turned away from Pisces, I was embarrassed, but strangely enough that reverse publicity worked well. Any place that would nix Paul Newman had to be something that everyone else wanted to get into, or so the townsfolk reasoned. Another inadvertent casualty of that ghastly night was late comedian Freddie Prinze, who also was unfortunately shown the curb when he made his bid.

Inaugurations are typically crowded, rowdy, messy events, but the bone-crusher at Pisces would never be repeated again, at least by me. Only divine Providence had kept our social disaster from being a catastrophe. Strained to the breaking point by the party, I had a feeling that 1977 was going to be a very strange year, indeed.

Chapter Ten

Koreagate was not as traumatic to the American public as the fall of Spiro Agnew, but when I glanced at the morning paper that turned a year's worth of rumors into headlines, I still shuddered. "Don't tell me . . . Zero for two!" I said to myself.

Even before the country put Tongsun's payoff problems on the front burner, I was preparing myself for trouble. I could see Pisces was not in any position to withstand the oncoming storm. The management company behind the club had never bounced back from its initial $80,000 deficit and its financial woes continued. On paper, it needed $100K immediately or the treasured waterfall, along with the rest, would dry up fast.

Park's assets in the United States were now frozen by the IRS for alleged back taxes owed. The original financial format of the management company called for each of the three partners to contribute extra needed capital proportionate to the share they owned. Our shortfall and desperately needed additional monies had been constantly discussed at board meetings. Since Park's 80 percent holding dominated, we were stymied as long as he remained out of the country and financially crippled.

It looked like the management company was going down the tubes. But coming up another pipe, a prominent local builder and a member of Pisces, Arpad Domyan, was putting the finishing touches on a suburban office complex for Time-Life Books and wanted to include a fancy restaurant. Domyan's idea was to center his restaurant on a socially oriented personality and he didn't have to look far. Was I interested?

For my front-man role, I was offered half of what the restaurant netted. The concept of a new Peter's in Alexandria, Virginia, was flexible and could function with or without my involvement at Pisces. The place would bear my signature as a logo, not only on the doors, but the dishes, menu, matches, and even promotional scarfs. To the world, it would be Peter's new place, as handsome as Pisces, but with no membership requirement and accessible to anyone willing to pay the price of a meal.

After a month and a half of fruitless board of directors meetings at Pisces, it was obvious the club had to do something fast. With the possibility of Peter's ready to bloom in the late spring, I was becoming increasingly short-tempered with Dickerson's complaints. Although he was president of the management company, I found myself criticized continually for the club's monetary mess. I was spending too much money wining and dining guests, I was told. There were too many "comp" drinks, too lavish a budget for flowers, too many cooks in the kitchen, and on and on. My contention held firm. "I never said I worked cheap! First-class P.R. costs an arm and a leg, but that's the name of the game. Why weren't these factors written in from the beginning!" So we bounced off each other endlessly.

On the surface, everything at Pisces was fine. When Spiro and Judy made their first and last visit to the club as my guests, everything was roses. Spiro spoke of his new business venture enthusiastically, and Judy was as warm and animated as ever. His scandal was forgotten at our table, and my problems, at least for two hours, didn't exist. It was a strange conversation in that our nostalgia was tainted and the future uncertain, but the present was full of congeniality.

In March, the week before Easter, I received a call from Tom Boggs. He had two complimentary Pan Am round-trip tickets for the company's inaugural flight to Australia. With the current mood in Washington, Boggs couldn't find a receptive congressman or dignitary to save his life. Everybody in town was afraid of being seen on a junket, although it was an honest, above-board P.R. offer. I dusted off my old Department of Commerce dignity, shined up my Pisces credentials, and said I'd be glad to go. "And the sooner the better, Tommy. Australia hardly sounds far enough away!"

A week into the trip I received a call from Wyatt, who reached me in Christchurch, New Zealand, where I was discovering the joys of herding sheep on a Moped. He was in an uproar. "We don't have any money for rent, Peter. The U.S. marshal is locking up the club on Friday!"

"Wyatt," I said impersonally, "you called me half the way around the world to tell me this. You're on the scene. You're the financial manager. Do something! I'll be in Bora Bora on Friday. If the club closes, let me know; and I'll extend my visit."

But even cynics worry about their "babies" and in my case it was Pisces. When I arrived back in the Capital, Wyatt had called for still another meeting. It was his contention that the management corporation should be put into bankruptcy, but the club itself would survive. In a nutshell, this meant the investors would lose, but the club could continue if someone new were brought in.

Wyatt was willing to put up "whatever monies necessary to keep the club afloat," he said. In return, he demanded that I step down as club president and that he be named in my place. He also wanted me to sell out the small interest I had. I thought he was asking for more than a pound of flesh and flatly refused in terms implying self-fornication.

It didn't take long for Tongsun Park's seconds-in-command to reach me. By not selling, they warned me, I was playing into Dickerson's hands. If the management company were allowed to fall into bankruptcy, Park's total investment in the club would be lost. In spite of the "TSP wheeler-dealer" accounts in the papers, it would be a thankless, ugly maneuver on my part to allow Park, a man who had fulfilled a fantasy of mine, to be thrown to the dogs. I was told that unless I went along with Dickerson, everybody had everything to lose.

I conferred with Tom Boggs and my personal friend and attorney Don Santarelli, a pair of pragmatists if there ever were any. They argued that I had little recourse other than to sell out. "Besides," Don said, "you're moving to Peter's anyway!"

There was far too much smoke in my eyes over this matter, as well as too many unanswered questions. A deal was cut whereby I would be retained by Pisces as a consultant until such time as I moved on. It was a travesty, with clauses about not having anything to do with press, and clearing all expenditures with Dickerson, etc., etc., etc. The arrangement lasted less than a month, at which time Peter's was ready to open.

Since you don't sabotage a dream that you've worked your

best to keep alive, rather than alienate my many friends who had joined and enjoyed Pisces, I held my tongue and carried on with my best smile. Except for the principals involved with the stock transfer, no one in the club or press knew that I had left with a broken arm. Peter's was opening and it was presumed that my exit was based on that.

But I was plagued with deep, personal misgivings and doubts. I've been at the P.R. roulette wheel a long time, and it seemed to me that I was jumping into a new restaurant too fast. I felt as if I had just been through a divorce and was running off with the first woman that said "yes." Also, I didn't trust Alexandria's provincial air, though I couldn't do much about where Domyan put his building. My name was on the door, but I wasn't sure whether I was ready for Old Town Alexandria and vice versa.

While I was turning these matters over in my mind, an old friend, who would help to give me some fresh perspectives, arrived in town. Since what seems like day one, Jack Haley, Jr., and I have been pals, literally growing up together. Some months before, he and his wife, Liza Minnelli, had come to Washington, where Liza was kicking off the gala season premiere of Wolf Trap, an outdoor performance center near Dulles Airport.

Jack flew in early and stayed with me in preparation for Liza's arrival. I had just taken a little flat off Embassy Row after giving up my McLean spread. I welcomed Jack's company, and we spent a good many hours reminiscing about old times in Hollywood, and by the time Liza arrived a few days before the show, my spirits had revived considerably.

On the night I first met her, I quickly learned that you cannot entertain Liza Minnelli. The opposite of a prima donna, Liza putzed around the house as much as Sinatra. While I made dinner, she followed behind like a sous-chef, cleaning-up, helping out, and looking for odd jobs to keep her busy. "Liza, go sit down and let *me* wait on *you*, for Christ's sake!" I'd wail. "Forget it, Malatesta! Where are the paper towels?" she'd snap back. After she cleared the table, she went back into the kitchen and reorganized the scattered trash in a big plastic garbage bag and dragged the works outside. Then, with the flat finally in order, we all plopped onto sofas and Jack and I filled her in with our rambling tales of long ago.

The next morning, a neighbor called me aside as I walked to

my car. "You know, Peter," she said, "your new maid is a dead-ringer for Liza Minnelli!"

"Isn't she?" I answered. "Know what? She sings too!"

Now, in the middle of my fretting about Peter's, Liza and Jack invited me to come to Manhattan for the premiere of *New York, New York.* Sanity said that this wasn't the best time for me to go off on such a junket, but no one had to twist my arm!

As soon as I got off the shuttle plane and saw the limo that Jack had sent, I had a feeling that this trip was going to be one for the books. They quartered me in a suite near theirs at the Sherry-Netherland Hotel, and we picked up where we had left off in Washington.

Jack was relaxed, Liza was as giddy as a little girl, and, to my chagrin, I found that I was the only one in the suite who was nervous about the opening. While I gingerly poured myself a small cure for the jitters, Liza, with an "Oh, come on!" air, grabbed the bottle and took a great swig out of it. No question of nerves there, just nonchalance.

The theater, filled with Jack and Liza's friends, gave the film a somewhat better reception than the critics. Sitting next to Liza during the screening, I tended to watch her reactions as much as the film. The mirror-effect of seeing a star observing herself perform is fascinating. In this case, Liza acted like everybody else. She somehow remained detached and enjoyed the character she played in the flick as if she were coming upon it for the first time.

After Liza had acknowledged the audience's enthusiastic applause, we high-tailed it to a party at the Rainbow Grill. Typical of Hollywood-New York opening night bashes, compliments and champagne prevailed. I noted that the film's director, Martin Scorsese, obviously had more than a professional liking for Liza; he reminded me of a little boy with a beard and a crush.

Liza's costar, Robert De Niro, spoke very little, but his bright, darting eyes gave away the fact that he, in his own withdrawn way, was having a good time just watching it all. At one point, he shyly introduced me to his father, the painter Robert De Niro. With bold, thrashing gestures, much like his oils, the elder De Niro enthused about young Robert's career and the "perpetual excitement of New York." I couldn't help laughing. "This is all backwards," I told him, "I thought painters were supposed to be moody and actors extroverted." For some reason, this observation seemed to delight him.

By 2:30 A.M., the limos lined-up and everyone was off to the hottest new club going, Studio 54. I had heard about it, with mixed reviews, but I was ready to see what this old, semirenovated TV studio had to offer.

As we arrived, I thought we were doing a rerun of the premiere a few hours earlier. Kids and screamers lined the block and paparazzi were everywhere. We were whisked into a fairly subdued lobby before entering a cavern of neon squiggles, red and white balloons, and the theme of *New York, New York* blaring at peak decibel levels. Literally hundreds of gorgeous kids, all worthy of a *Vogue* or *GQ* cover, yelled, danced, paraded, stared, and whispered. Off in dark corners or buried in cliques, I noticed Halston, Calvin Klein, and Andy Warhol holding court. Christina Onassis, surrounded by admirers, swirled by, and in her wake straggled a young man who looked like a star-struck preppie. This, I was told, was Steve Rubell, 54's owner. I thought I had seen it all, but I had to admit to myself that this Rubell kid had a social gold mine that humbled our little operation in Georgetown. A different set of players, of course, but I'd have traded my act for his anytime!

Studio 54, for a newcomer, was overwhelming; after twenty minutes, I stepped outside for a gasp of air, only to see the street still mobbed and boisterous with people who just wanted to be *near* the place. No doubt about it: This West Side celebrity hangout was the hottest nightclub in the whole damn country, and I grew greener at the thought of returning to Alexandria after this taste of hi-tech Sodom and Gomorrah. Oh boy! I mused, I get to order the kitchen supplies tomorrow.

Old Town is a speedy seven miles from Washington, but it might as well be 1,000. Nothing like Peter's had ever opened there, and in starting, the new place had as many cost overruns as Pisces. But I made an about-face when I took stock of a potentially wonderful new opportunity.

The emphasis of the operation was again on glamor. Sleek, Marlboro red banquettes gave the place a Manhattan feel. Its airy, five-story atrium gave Peter's a sophisticated, almost tropical air. It was full of allusions to Pisces—with fish tanks, palms, dim candlelight, a European menu, and wall upon wall of Warhol lithographs. Championing local artists, as well, I commissioned Eric Moody to create a 2,000-piece Tiffany stained-glass mosaic depicting landmark

Old Town buildings. The antique oak, oval bar under it was reminiscent of Toots Shor's in New York.

The restaurant reviewers called it "handsome and clubbish," "superb," "definitely worthy of a Saturday night," and so on, although a few balked at the idea of charging Alexandrians an average of $25 a head for dinner.

One food critic was surprised to see well-known members of Pisces eating dinner at Peter's in their shirtsleeves and, occasionally, tennis shoes. All that mattered to me was the fact that they were willing to truck across the Potomac and give the place a chance. It was an exciting and, for Alexandria, unique nightspot that didn't need to be reached by driving into Washington. Unfortunately, it also held true that Washington didn't need to drive all the way out to Alexandria for that kind of sparkle.

After the trumpets and flourishes of the successful first month, the business tapered a bit. Although Peter's captivated the local press, which ran color pictures of the bar on its front page, it didn't exactly set the town on fire. We did a fair and steady business, but the overhead needed to maintain a place like this was formidable. Peter's had to pack them in on a large scale every night or the numbers just weren't going to fall into place.

Yet, business considerations apart, I found I sometimes rather enjoyed Peter's on quiet nights. It was a refreshing refuge from the incessant political warfare of Washington. Tongsun Park, once he quietly returned to testify, would sometimes take an obscure corner table. Spiro enjoyed the food and the place's low-keyed atmosphere. Ron Ziegler, the front man in the Nixonian war with the press, would sit at the bar. Hamilton Jordan, "exiled" from Georgetown because of the Amaretto-spitting incident, took refuge at Peters as if it were the last place the gossip columnists would look. Bert Lance, still stinging from his own problems, would catch dinner there rather than face the stares and gossip of the city. Thus, among other things, Peter's was a sort of haven for the politically wounded. If you judge a man by his company, I was a controversial restaurateur if there ever was one. "I wonder why John Mitchell hasn't stopped by?" I once asked my bartender.

While nearly every one of my Embassy Row and social friends at one time or another came in to enjoy dinner and wish the place well, I could hardly claim to have drawn that crowd on a regular basis. Peter's was too far away from Washington. "They just won't cross that damn bridge," I moaned. But I had known all along that Alexandria never was, and never would be, on Washington's social turf. The frontier was laid out years ago and, with the exception of country clubs, the suburbs never amounted to anything more, socially, than a place to live.

It was obvious to one reporter that Peter's was not doing well, and when he quizzed me on it, I replied, "Running Peter's in Alexandria is like trying to put Rive Gauche in Beltsville. This town's like Brigadoon: It comes along once every hundred years."

The comment caused a furor in little old Alexandria, although my phone was ringing off the hook with congratulatory calls from fellow cynics in D.C. The newspaper received a watered down, ambiguous apology from me the next day. Not that I was sorry—I'm incorrigible; but business was bad enough without irking the locals.

Meanwhile, Arpad Domyan was becoming restless. Although we both had known from the onset that the business would need at least two years to mature into a highly profitable operation, he was unhappy with the statistics after six months. So was I. Once again, I was undercapitalized in a venture that depended upon long-term growth, and I was becoming increasingly frustrated. Like Jordan, Lance, Agnew, and Park, I found myself using Alexandria as a refuge, but there was at least one important difference: My exile was self-inflicted and, at bottom, unnecessary. Still, hanging on the thinnest of threats, Domyan and I decided to give Peter's one final go.

I received a phone call from Dolores Hope in mid-April asking about the seating capacity and availability of Peter's. She wanted to hold Bob's seventy-fifth birthday at the restaurant the night before he was officially honored at the Kennedy Center. A White House reception was scheduled on the same day as the "family" birthday party, so careful timing and preparation and a smooth operation were essential. Dolores' guest list was staggering, and her gesture of faith in my supper club was touching. We both knew Peter's could certainly use a shot in the arm, and if that crowd couldn't provide it, it was time to take down the shingle once and for all. And by the same token, I was anxious to please *them.* I now had a chance, after all these years, to reciprocate the graciousness she and Bob had always extended to me. I was determined to make this event a success.

Perhaps I went overboard. Days in advance, the staff began working long hours on the menu. The restaurant, although still new, had to be freshened up, and the decorations, flowers, invitations, and security all needed to be coordinated; and for the overall decor, I flew in Beverly Hills designer Laura Mako to lend her unique touch. Meanwhile, I fretted over miniscule details like shiny waiters' shoes and perfectly pressed napkins. Were the bottles on the bar lined up straight? Is the birthday card drawing of Bob here yet? Did we have a ramp for Omar Bradley's wheelchair? How many more balloons would it take to cover the ceiling? I doubt that Nixon, Agnew, Sinatra, or Park had ever seen me work so hard on any single project.

The final twelve hours before the event were the worst. I functioned with a phone in each hand and a go-fer by my side all day. Without thinking twice, I turned down an invitation to the afternoon affair for Hope at the White House so I could put a few extra hours in with the chef. By six o'clock, no use to anyone any more, I crawled home to wash my face, change clothes, and try to gather my wits. With the Carter social not breaking up until seven, I dillydallied for a while, staring at my puffy, exhausted face in the bathroom mirror. I dragged myself back to the restaurant by a quarter to seven, with fifteen minutes to spare.

The apparition of Lucy doing her imitation of a maitre d' told me I was too late—the party had already begun.

Like any party, this one was a composite of many things—some frivolous, some serious. It was the first time Elizabeth Taylor and Hope had ever sat together at a dinner table. Liz told me later that she had looked forward to this moment for years, and Bob joked that from now on if he got any calls from "an Elizabeth, be sure to get the last name." But beneath Hope's banter, there was an undertone of sadness, for Bing Crosby had just died. Another guest who particularly felt Crosby's loss was Dorothy Lamour, whose feelings were compounded by the fact that her own husband had just passed away as well. Her bravery as she held back tears affected everyone close to her.

But there was much gaiety, too. Jim Henson and Frank Oz had left their Muppets back at the Kennedy Center, but how we howled when the famous voices of Miss Piggy and Kermit teased the crowd. Charles Nelson Reilly's cutups as he held court at one end of the bar annihilated the guy pouring drinks.

Some guests, like David Soul and Elliott Gould, I had never met before, but I quickly learned to admire the gumption and civic-mindedness of today's new breed of actors. And, of course, there was Omar Bradley, the only living five-star general, whose charm and keen intelligence made the facts of his advanced age and wheelchair seem irrelevant.

Pearl and Dolores took their turns singing and I realized what a genuine family this mix was, what close bonds these seemingly diverse people had! This party was their way of standing up and being counted as people who loved Hope and believed in what he represented. But Hope saw to it that I didn't get carried away by sentiment. At one point, he quipped, "Peter's Place—sounds like a waiting room of a gynecologist's office."

I have other confused memories of the evening—of Carol Lawrence arriving late from a rehearsal, starving and digging into a plate of pasta as though it would save her life—of noticing that Stu Symington and Westy Westmoreland rather resembled one another and thinking how little either had aged—of remembering that I had played golf with Fred MacMurray fully thirty years before on the Loyola University golf team and thinking that he, too, had hardly changed.

The reporters were already beginning to say nice things while the party was still in progress. With each compliment, I gazed back at Dolores, knowing all along that once again she had been responsible for my success. And only I knew it, for, as usual, she took no credit, wanting the spotlight to fall on me.

The subsequent newspaper accounts astounded Domyan, and as business increased, riding the brief wave of glamor that publicity provides, it looked again like Peter's might stay on solid ground. But it was not to be.

Three months later, Peter's was divided into two parcels. One half became additional Time-Life offices; the other, a bar and grill with a different name and host. I finally got the year off that I yearned for since the day I went to Linda's wedding instead of taking my sailboat around the world.

A decade of parties and politics had come to an end. But not really an end, since I'll never willingly cut my ties with this particular kind of socializing. For a certain kind of person—and I guess I'm one of them—the Washington party circuit exercises an irresistible fascination. I may never again be able to aspire to be one of the great Washington hosts, but to be honest, I'd like to be one. Parties anywhere can be glamorous and exciting, but only in Washington do they have that special, exhilarating undertone of potency—that ever-present sense that from a casual conversation between guests or from some brief chance meeting, matters of national consequence might flow.

So I'm hooked. And I'll always be hooked. And not for a moment will I ever regret it.

Epilogue

The closest I ever got to that trip around the world was six months of watching early morning reruns of TV's *Love Boat.* The relative solitude of my condominium in Washington gave me time to shed twenty pounds, unpack the bags under my eyes, and take a good look at dozens of cardboard boxes, crowded with notes, letters, memorabilia, news clippings, and invitations. Somewhere in that mess, there was a story.

The dog walkers in Bancroft Park must have thought I was crazy as I sat at a weather-beaten picnic table, mumbling endlessly into a cassette recorder. The telephone went unanswered as I plowed through scribbled diaries, and crisp, new invitations sat unopened on my desk. The cool autumn nights were no longer surrendered to embassy buffets, as I pounded out my first few vignettes, far more worried about where to put a comma than I ever had been about where to seat His Excellency's wife. After years of relentless party chatter, I often found myself staring at a viciously blank page.

At one point, I called Andy Warhol, both to refresh a sometimes blurred memory and to find out whom I could turn to with my sixty crudely typed, dog-eared pages. Andy was cautious, saying he knew a great agent, one of the best, but a tough cookie who knew her business, named Roz Cole. He told me I could give her a call, but that I'd have to listen to whatever she said. He warned, "If she doesn't like it, you might as well pack it up early and try another profession."

New York was a blustery, snowed-in mess that day in January. Cross-country skiers were darting from frozen, silent Fifth

Avenue as if all Manhattan were a hilltop in Vermont. I trudged through the snowbanks on the way to 21, clutching my fat manila envelope of selected memories, unsure if any of this was going to lead to anything. It had been a while, but Jimmy at 21 still remembered my favorite table. The normally busy restaurant was nearly deserted, and the staff was more than usually attentive, but I waved away the wine list automatically: This was to be a business lunch, I hoped.

After polishing off my second Perrier, I was still a shade nervous. What do I say to her? I mused, fingering the envelope while I waited. This was just like the time Hope left me alone in the locker room to make conversation with Ike. . . . Oh, my God! How could I forget to write that story? . . . I'll just tell it to her and write it later.

"Peter Malatesta? Hi. I'm Roz Cole."

I looked up from my worry and found a tiny, intelligent-looking woman with a business-like tone in her voice.

"I'm here at this luncheon because your friend Andy Warhol told me I should meet you. Let's have a drink and find out what you're going to offer." No vice president or movie star had ever been that blunt on a hello.

A little taken aback, I fumbled with the material and said, "Roz, I've had a very interesting ten years, and I've put down some of it. There might be something here that could be enjoyable reading about how the worlds of politics and parties mix."

She tilted her head as if to say, "Yeah, well so what?"

"Andy tells me you're the best agent for people who are writing this stuff. I've always had a fantasy in my life about writing a book. Do you think we can pull it off?"

She gave me a quizzical look, and then settled back in her chair to listen to my story.